Snakes

Dedication

To Janet
my friend and my neighbour
without whom
this book would not have happened

STEPHEN VERNEY

Snakes and Ladders

To Becca with
Love from
Sandra (and Stephen †)

Christmas 2022.

First published in Great Britain in 2016 by Verney Books

ISBN 978-0-9926856-2-1

CONTENTS

࿐

FOREWORD
Sandra Verney

৻৶৽৻

Stephen spent the last ten years of his life writing this book. It was to be a coming together of the ideas and emotions which he had been entertaining for almost 90 years. It was an exhilarating and painful process, and when he died, the main body of the book was complete, and meticulously recorded by his great friend and neighbour, Janet Wagon, who had patiently redrafted and collated a number of different versions over the years. The Introduction was in note form only, but Stephen had had deep discussions about its content with me and many other people. So here I am, trying to tell you what we talked about for endless hours, at home on winter evenings, out gardening on summer days, and sitting in the car as we travelled.

There are three images which inspired Stephen to write this book.

The first was the game of Snakes and Ladders which he played as a child. You threw the dice, and if you landed at the foot of a ladder, you went up to the top. If you landed at the mouth of a snake, you slid down through the snake's belly and ended up at the tip of his tail.

The second image was Jacob's dream of a ladder between heaven and earth, on which angels go up and down in a two way traffic [Genesis 28]. The word for 'ladder' in the original Greek is 'climax', and anyone who has used a ladder knows that being at the top soon becomes an anticli-max if, for some reason, you can't come down again.

The third image came when Stephen started to study theology. It was the description of Paradise, in 'The Vision of God', a book written by Nicholas of Cusa in 1453 AD.

Paradise was a walled garden, and the wall was made up of opposites. An angel with a bright sword kept guard over these ramparts. The name of the angel was Reason, and Reason would not allow any human being to enter because they could not hold opposites together. Love lived within the walls, and Love was able to hold together these opposites, and enable us humans to do the same.

These images highlight the 'opposites' that we all have to struggle with on our journey from childhood to old age, and I now hand you over to Stephen so that you can join him on his journey.

PART 1

CHILDHOOD

❦

My father was a man brimful of energy, in whom spirituality and politics overlapped. He was influenced in his childhood by his great aunt, Florence Nightingale, to whom his father's father had proposed marriage. When she refused him, he had married her sister, Parthenope, and Florence, in later life, lived with them in Claydon House, the Verney family home in Buckinghamshire. There were frequent one to one meetings between 'the old lady and the little boy' and he carried with him throughout his life the inspiration of her radical compassion and her unique sense of humour, together with the more baleful influences of her obsessive overworking.

He was also a man of wide interests. He loved the poetry of Robert Browning and used to read it aloud at family gatherings. He conducted the village choral society with his own colourful enthusiasm. He enjoyed jokes and funny stories, especially with his children. There were 8 of us, and he taught his 5 boys to play cricket and football, having himself been a soccer blue at Oxford. He taught all 8 of us to feel at home in the sea in Anglesey – just to float and let the sea support us and then to swim. I mention Anglesey in particular, because every summer there was a mass exit from Claydon, when the whole family went to Rhoscolyn, our family home near Holyhead. Huge excitement as we all climbed into a little train at Verney Junction. First stop Bletchley, where our train was hooked on to a main line train to Anglesey. On arrival at Holyhead there was even more excitement when we saw the array of horses and carts which transported us to Rhoscolyn, where our summer really began.

In 1910 my father had been elected as a Liberal MP and became a Junior Minister in Asquith's government. Asquith was replaced by Lloyd George in 1916 after a wartime vote of confidence. But early in 1918 my father voted against Lloyd George when he knew that the truth had not been told. For this he was punished at the end of the war when Lloyd George ran a candidate against him in the general election, and he was defeated while still abroad in the Middle East.

Then in April 1926 there was a by-election which marks for me the transition from childhood to boyhood. My father was standing as Liberal candidate for the Buckrose constituency in Yorkshire, and soon after my 7th birthday the whole family moved up to Bridlington to support him. It was an exciting time, and we were all gripped by election fever. Aunt Ellin wrote 'The conversation was of nothing else, even amongst the nursery party. Stephen confided, 'You know – long ago – but I thought – a general election meant that Father got in everywhere'.' There were now 8 children, with Lawrence aged 2 and Catherine aged 4 months; we older children, that is to say down to Andrew aged 4, used to go to the beach every day to construct election posters with big stones, in a position that would attract the attention of passers by.

One of them read **V**ote for
Verney and
Victory

We also composed election songs to be sung to well known tunes.

> Come and vote for Verney
> We'll put Sir Harry in,
> Every vote is wanted
> Because we're going to win.

Lloyd George came up to support us and shook hands with all of us children in front of the camera, but in spite of all of our efforts, wider events moved to defeat my father. The general strike was called, and upper and middle class England was in a panic with volunteers enrolling to do the strikers' work. My father persevered against all pressures, and on polling day he was defeated by only 2000 votes by Mr Braithwaite, the Conservative candidate, who was to us children a bogey man representing the forces of darkness. But we carried on playing 'Elections' – our favourite childhood game. Each of us had a fictitious name and we held our own hustings in the Cedar Room at Claydon, on the beach at Rhoscolyn or anywhere else where we happened to be.

After his election defeat, my father continued to play the game of politics, but in a different way. In spite of his original spirit, he was a prisoner of the masculine power game. For him, the House of Commons would always be the best club in the world, but now he decided to throw himself into the world of business. He became Director of a number of companies, including the vigorous Marks and Spencer. At the same time, having always been a keen churchman, he took on a leading role as a radical in The Church Assembly.

He was a man of his time, who took it for granted that men should lead and women should follow. But in his private life this attitude was confused by his own personal lack of self esteem. He had grown up as the only boy in a family with three powerful elder sisters, a mother who was a distinguished public figure and a father, whom, as he once confessed to me, he experienced as 'an awful man'. His memories of prep school at the age of 8 were of the Headmaster bullying him physically by pressing his head backwards until he confessed to having said the word 'damn' – which, in fact, someone else had said; and the Art Master at the same school saying to him

'Verney, you are the ugliest little boy I have ever taught'. All this became a powerful background to his marriage. He adored my mother but, at the same time, felt inferior to her. His emotional development had been frozen at an early age, and throughout his life, in spite of his huge charisma, he was haunted by his longing to be the pretty little boy that teachers would like, and was tormented by his craving for success and approval.

I remember my mother as a pool of stillness. Bubbling up from the depth of the pool was happiness and a love that seemed to flow out of a source where she knew Love in the centre of herself. This Love overflowed into the practicalities of keeping house – she had a wonderful way of using words, such as 'I got my sleeves into Claydon'. This Love also manifested itself in the way she cherished her family – on arrival at Rhoscolyn, where the house and its contents were damp after winter, she would wear our vests herself to make sure that they were aired and she always made sure that the towels and ginger biscuits were ready and waiting for us after we had bathed in the sea. I remember her secretly showing me a bird's nest with a cluster of little eggs and telling me the names of the flowers growing in the high hedgerows as we walked home from the beach. She taught me to know by heart the parables of the Prodigal Son and the Good Samaritan before I could read, and when I wanted to detain her at bedtime I would say 'Tell me about God' – which I knew would be difficult for her to resist.

Her history, which I found out later, was that she was one of eleven children born to the 9th Earl of Elgin, who became Viceroy of India when she was four years old. This meant that her parents were away for the next five years of her childhood, and when they came back, her mother was an invalid. Her family home was Broomhall near Dunfermline, where she was surrounded by the portraits of her ancestors and the sword of Robert the Bruce. Her grandfather, James, the 8th Earl, was a sensitive and intelligent man, who became a distinguished empire builder, first as Governor General of Canada which he virtually created as an entity; then as Commander in Chief of the British Forces in the far east where, against his own vision of mutual respect between East and West, he had to invade China and sack the Summer Palace of the Emperor; and finally as Governor General of India where he became Queen Victoria's first Viceroy. He was one of the outstanding characters of his generation, as his father Thomas, the 7th Earl, had been one of the most notorious characters of the previous generation. Thomas, a complex and artistic man was appointed British Ambassador to the Turkish Caliphate at a dangerous moment when Napoleon was set on conquering Egypt. He took his own artist and his own little private orchestra with him to Constantinople. During a visit to Athens he noticed that many of the fine marble statues on the Parthenon were being destroyed by the Turkish Army, and he decided to rescue them. Others, including Byron, say that he plundered them and that Scotland should be ashamed of him: 'Blush, Caledonia! Such thy son could be'. Be that as it may, the Elgin Marbles finished up in the British Museum, but Elgin himself was ruined financially since the government never refunded him for their transport nor even paid him for his years as ambassador.

So my mother grew up with this heritage of illustrious ancestors, and without the support of her parents for five years, but miraculously free of the psychological problems which this might have created. She was a happy child, at peace with herself, and in sympathy with other people and the natural world around her. Spiritually, she grew up within the Presbyterian Kirk of Scotland with its deep love and respect for the Bible, and it was as though the absence of her parents became a doorway through which she had discovered 'Our Father who art in heaven', and the personal presence of Jesus Christ with whom she could know that heavenly father here on earth. There was nothing pietistic or exclusive about her spirituality; she found it natural to be both earthy and heavenly at the same time.

This wholeness grew out of her image of God, as William Blake describes it in his Songs of Innocence, in a little poem called *The Divine Image* which ends

> Where mercy, love, and pity dwell,
> There God is dwelling too.

Arising out of the same image of God was the remarkable fact that when she saw God's will she did it. My father used to quote the prayer 'Grant that we may both perceive and know what things we ought to do, and also may have grace and power faithfully to fulfil the same'. He would say to us children, 'I know what I ought to do, but I find it difficult to fulfil the same. Your mother sometimes has trouble with the first, but once she perceives and knows what she ought to do, she has the grace and the power to do it'.

My father said that his wife was a saint – and in a sense she was – *a human being fully alive in the moment.* But he projected on to her the illusory perfection of an angel who wears a halo and occupies the high moral ground; he polarised them, she the saint and he the sinner, and in consequence he felt threatened by her and found her saintliness difficult to live with. He compensated by asserting himself through a ceaseless round of being busy and always in a hurry – after all, his Headmaster had taught him at an early age that if you delayed in any way there would be painful and humiliating consequences. Every time our family went out together my father would be early at the door looking at his watch and getting exasperated while my mother would be attending to some final duty of housekeeping, or helping one of us to find a missing garment. We nicknamed our parents Sir Harry Hurry-up and The Lady Rachel Presently.

Now, in retrospect, I see that children inherit both of their parents, and that they have to live any opposites according to their own unique personality, as do I and my 7 brothers and sisters. My parents called each other 'Oney' – to rhyme with honey and after their death, Simon Verity carved on their tombstone, two clasped hands.

In a poem by Wallace Stevens, called *How to live and what to do,* he describes a man and his companion climbing a great mountain.

Those two remind me of my father and mother; for us children they were a ladder between time and eternity.

9

They stopped to rest before the heroic height.
Coldly the wind fell on them.
In many majesties of sound;
There was neither voice nor created image,
No chorister nor priest.
There was only the height of the rock
And the two of them standing still to rest.
There was the cold wind and the sound it made
Away from the muck of the land that they had left,
Heroic sound, joyous and jubilant and sure.

Through the life and death of our parents many of us have heard the sound of that wind.

RUMOURS OF WAR

჻

I went up to Balliol College, Oxford, in October 1937.

For the next two years, one question predominated over every other; would there be a war against Hitler's Germany?

He had annexed the Rhineland in 1936, and Austria in 1937. His next move would probably be into Czechoslovakia or Poland. Then we would be bound to go to their help. Conscription would be imposed, and war declared.

The question then arose, should we join up in the armed forces, or should we declare ourselves to be conscientious objectors? This was not a theoretical problem for the future. We, as young men of 20, would be in the first call up, and we should have to choose between the way of pacifism, or of joining in the armed resistance to Hitler.

As a Christian, I was inclined towards the first choice, as were many of my contemporaries. I found it impossible to imagine Jesus opening fire with a machine gun, or dropping bombs on his enemies; his way seemed to be the exact opposite – the way of powerlessness and forgiveness – to die rather than to kill.

But I began to understand the opposite argument in January 1938 when I went on a skiing holiday to Austria. There, in a public park, I saw a park bench, and on it a notice which said 'Jews Forbidden'. The sheer inhumanity of this made my blood run cold – and I knew it was only the tip of a terrible iceberg. Who was I, and who were my friends at Oxford, that we should keep our hands clean of the atrocities of war, while a mad dictator wreaked his ever more unspeakable atrocities on these helpless people?

Jesus was saying to us 'Follow me'. But which of these ways did he want us to go? Or did he, somehow, hold them together within himself – so that he could say 'I AM the way? Follow ME.

I determined that in the long vacation of 1938 I would go to Czechoslovakia, and, as far as possible, see at first hand what was really happening. I found a kindred spirit in Madron Seligman, whom I had known both at school and at college, and who was keen to come with me. He brought another dimension of concern and perhaps of danger into our exploration because of his Jewish background.

We set off on July 13th, and passed through Dresden where we spent a few hours looking at pictures and palaces. We met with courtesy everywhere. The only blot was the Jewish persecution. We saw that most of the shops were labelled 'Aryan', and occasionally one had a big notice – 'A Jewish Shop'.

But when we arrived at Prague, we found ourselves in the middle of an acute crisis that had been hanging over the Czechs all that summer. I wrote to my parents, 'It appears that May 1st was the first date fixed by Hitler for the invasion. All the bunting and the decorations were made ready by the Henlein party, and the streets were to be renamed Hitlerstrasse and Göringstrasse. The next date was May 15th, when Czech men were called out of bed and hurried through the darkness to their frontier posts. Now they believe that they might not be invaded until after the German harvest was in, and that the invasion, when it came, would be through Austria. Chamberlain's statements of policy suggests that there would be active support from England.'

The next day we moved from our hotel into the YMCA

which was cheaper, and where we found ourselves part of an interesting community, including journalists and refugees. Here, I began to hear it expressed that British foreign policy was very much despised, and particularly Chamberlain. Also, that in the case of war, America would certainly come in, as she did in the last war, to protect her capitalist interests.

A day or two later, we took our rucksacks and went walking in the north of the country, the Sudeten German area. We looked in as often as possible to a pub, both to enjoy a glass of beer but also to have a conversation about the political situation. Our leading question to the publican was always 'Are you all German around here?', and this, we found, led to a stream of vituperation and threats against the Czechs. They were 95% German, and they wanted autonomy, but they knew they would not get it without a war. The most interesting meeting was with a German, aged about 35, and his wife. He was a well educated business-man, very charming and intelligent; we talked for a time about sport, and then asked our inevitable question. He began slowly to explain the situation, but as he went on, his face grew red, he clenched his fists, his eyes glowed and his voice rose. 'For 20 years', he said 'the Germans have been oppressed. The Czechs are good democrats to their own people, but they treat the Germans like foreigners. Czech is a very difficult language to learn and Germans cannot master it. Whenever I visit officials, they refuse to speak German, even in the German speaking areas. The Czechs do not wish to understand the Germans and resent the fact that their fate seems to be bound up with Germany. I am a democrat, and I abhor fascism, but rather than continue like this, I would welcome Hitler, who is, before all else, a German,'

By the time we got back to Prague, I had become aware of the two sides of the problem. I was, too, becoming disillusioned about diplomacy, and about British diplomats. I wrote to my parents, 'We have visited the British Consul and Vice Consul, and a more worthy pair of empire-builders you could not imagine. They have, neither of them, bothered to learn the language or understand the people. The Consul spoke a lot about India and believed that what was good enough for Britain was good enough for India. This seems to be their attitude about the rest of Europe.

'I argued with him for an hour, and I am afraid that he is now rather worried about the decadence of modern youth. It obviously is no good to argue with that sort of man.'

In the next few days, that criticism of our diplomats was confirmed, at the highest level of power politics, and at the same time, by a coincidence of opposites, I would see the way of forgiveness and powerlessness, which had beckoned us, back in Oxford, as perhaps the true way of Jesus.

The 'opposites' involved, on the one hand, the decision of the British Government to send Lord Runciman to Prague, as a mediator; and on the other, my own encounter at the foot of a staircase, with a lame man called Klatchkin.

The first of those opposites was drawn to my attention by a letter from my father, who urged me to write and offer my services to the Runciman Mission. When Lord Runciman was in the cabinet under Asquith's government, my father, then an MP, had been his Private Secretary. I duly wrote to Runciman, but at the same time I wrote a deeply pessimistic letter to my father – 'We send out Lord Runciman, write conciliatory and flattering letters about Hitler, and all the time we are like children playing under a mountain and bolstering up an avalanche with sand castles, There is such a mess out here, that only a war, or a religious revival, can possibly clear things up, and there is no sign of the latter. I believe that a war is coming. Personally, I think that Lord Runciman can do nothing about it.'

Then, within the depths of my pessimism, the opposites coincided – those opposites of which we were becoming conscious in Oxford, and which I had come to Czechoslovakia to explore.

In a letter to my Father dated August 9th 1938, I wrote, 'Two hours ago, I met a lame man walking down a staircase and he stopped at the bottom to ask me something. He spoke in English and we started a conversation, which has only just finished. His name is Klatchkin. His father was Irish and his mother Russian. He is 33. At the age of 9 he was badly wounded in Ireland, in the troubles, and has been lame ever since. He has spent many years in China and is a Chinese subject. Lately he has been living in Germany. Two days ago he arrived here without any money, after 6 months in a German prison, on a charge of which he was finally acquitted – 6 months, he says, which were worse than death – and he left Germany in case it should happen again. On arrival here, he bought with his last money, a kilogram of sugar on which he has been living ever since.

'That is the setting for our conversation; and you will probably expect that we talked violently and heatedly about fascism. But no. He spoke in a way that I can only describe as 'the logic of love'. He spoke quietly with arguments that showed both his intellect and modesty. This man, starving and exiled, insisted that only through understanding and sympathy with the other side could good come out of evil; that we must live from the positive standpoint, seeking God through what is good. But it was not a sermon; it was, rather, a Socratic dialogue, interspersed with literary criticisms and foreign religions and customs. I cannot write any more now, I must rush off and give him food.'

Two days later, on August 11th, I wrote again to my father, describing the other opposite. 'Yesterday morning [the day after meeting Klatchkin], I found the enclosed letter from Lady Runciman. You can imagine how excited I was, and the rest of the day was spent polishing my boots and brushing the creases out of my suit. Then about 4 o'clock I had a shower bath and put on the special shirt that I had kept for an occasion, and walked slowly [so as not to sweat] to the hotel.

'His Lordship was in the lounge signing papers. I took the lift up to Lady Runciman, who received me very abruptly, as I had been led to expect from your letter. I passed a rather uncomfortable five minutes under a barrage of questions, most of which she answered herself. His Lordship then appeared with Lady Bonham Carter. He was most charming to me, very kind, distinguished and wise, but after about two minutes, he had to go away to work, and all that I had managed to tell him was that I did not speak Czech. Had I been able to, I might have got a job,

'I was now left alone with the two ladies, and felt very much *de trop*. They were old friends, and talked of Willie and Edward and the Hays and Prince Schwarzberg, while I sat nervously on the edge of my chair, tittering at the jokes and, otherwise, quite unable to join in. Every now and then Lady Runciman would turn suddenly upon me and flash out a question. 'Do you shoot?' 'Do you ride?' 'What are you going to be?' to which the answers had to be 'No' 'No' and 'I don't know'. After each answer, she seemed to look at me with increased contempt, and turned back, with a shudder, to Lady Bonham Carter. I was obviously not the right man for his Lordship.

'The conversation then turned to politics. I leant forward eagerly. Now was my chance to show my grasp of the problem. Lady Bonham Carter and Lady Runciman spoke of all foreigners with haughty condescension. Lady Runciman had gathered her views from German and Czech aristocracy, and did not seem to understand the problem that was to be solved, far less to have any idea of a solution. She gives the appearance of leading the Runciman Mission; if she really does so, God help us all. I tried, very objectively, with facts I have collected and from conversations that I have had with the working people, to hint to the noble lady that she might have made a slip or two and overlooked certain details of the situation. But any data that upset her were prejudged conclusions which she refused to believe as true. I think she is a kindly old thing at heart, but her manner is so aggressive that I found it impossible to know how to behave. I left, feeling a failure.'

Two days later [August 13th] I wrote again to my father, 'I am preparing to leave Prague for a few days walking in the High Tatras, which is said to be the most beautiful mountain scenery in central Europe. I shall be sorry to leave Klatchkin. He calls me *liebes Kind* [dear child], but in fact, I have become almost a father to him. He is in a state of nervous breakdown after his hurried flight from Germany, and his childhood wounds are causing him great pain. I took him to a hospital yesterday, but nothing could be seen from an x-ray. Outwardly, he is a wreck of a man, but when he starts talking, his ugly and mis-shapen face seems to brighten, and I sit enthralled at his feet. He has lived a dreadful life of suffering, but it has created a splendid

character. He is a poet, a painter and he writes music. He is
a philosopher, a literary critic and a student of humanity. He
has used his life of sickness to study questions for which the
healthy person has no time. He offered to teach me German,
but I am always so excited by what he is saying that we have
to speak English,'

Meanwhile, the international tension was increasing.
Before we left Oxford, the Financial Adviser to the Cabinet
had said to us that there was a 1-2 chance of war in August,
when Germany had got the harvest in. Now, we were reading
in the papers that in Germany, every man had been turned on
to getting the harvest in, and that next week 1,300,000
Germans would be taking part in army manoeuvres on the
Czechoslovakian frontier. Among the Sudetendeutsch it was
being whispered that August 15th would be 'the day' – or
perhaps August 25th.

I walked in the Tatras with another friend from Balliol,
and then spent the last week of our holiday with him,
looking at the art in Prague. In my last letter home on
August 24th, I wrote:

'The chief impression that I am carrying away with me is
of admiration for Prague and its art. I hope Hitler has no real
power against the real genius of this country. In Prague, with
its riot of beauty that sweeps through the centuries in a
cascade of inspiration, there lives a spirit that no guns can
conquer; and that spirit today is alive and vigorous.

'If I say anything about the politics, it is an afterthought –
an afterthought, however, that makes me feel hot. I have
heard rumours of a second Hore-Laval pact; only, this time,
it will be Runciman, Daladier and Chamberlain, and the
victims will be sold to the butcher Hitler. German army
manoeuvers are a gigantic bluff; but Chamberlain is fright-

ened, and has agreed to sell the Czechs to save his own skin. He wants, at all costs, to prevent a war – for once it starts, France is pledged, and we must go with her.

'England may be preparing for one of the most perfidious actions of her whole history, and I am fond enough of my country to be disturbed about it'.

When we got back to Oxford, my forebodings were immediately confirmed. Chamberlain went to visit Hitler at Berchtesgaden on September 15th, and again at Godesberg on September 22nd. Finally, Chamberlain and Daladier met Hitler and Mussolini at Munich on September 29th, and an agreement was signed to guarantee Czechoslovakia against further aggression. Chamberlain arrived back in England, waving a piece of paper which ensured peace in our time. A few days later, on October 4th, Hitler's troops invaded the Sudetenland.

Immediately, I was caught up in a wave of protest. There was to be a by-election in Oxford, and the Master of Balliol, A D Lindsay, one of the finest and wisest men in Oxford, decided to stand as an opposition candidate. He spoke to the college and said, 'I have gone mad, but that is no reason that you should all go mad too ... From every point, it is wrong for the head of a college to stand for parliament, but circumstances are just so, that I have to do it, and there is nothing more to be said. So I would like to say, very seriously, to you, to carry on with your work, and leave me to my madness'. I could not take this advice, and canvassed for him. He lost by a substantial majority.

The government introduced conscription for 20 and 21 year old men on April 27th of the following year. I wrote to my parents, 'There is a cloud of anxiety over the college today. The medical students are searching the papers for news of their exemption. The army men are wondering whether service in the OTC will see them through, and others have made a last minute dash for the Territorials. And what am I doing myself? I really hardly know. Alternatively laughing and crying. From Chamberlain's point of view it is surely right. If he is going to have commitments, he must have an army. For myself, I am considering whether to offer my services as a Red Cross worker.'

Then, on June 3rd, came the day of decision. I write in my diary, 'I signed the CO [conscientious objectors] register, or rather, asked permission to be put on it. So we have come to grips at last. I have, next, to fill in a form stating my reasons for applying for this permission, which I send to a tribunal ... the whole problem is very painful. I cannot sign cheerfully on either side, as so many seem able to do. By refusing to fight, I do feel that I am betraying a lot of good people whom I have a duty to defend. I am sure it is not a light thing, and that we pacifists are immoral and selfish if we shut our eyes to the fact that we are trying to subvert the social framework, without which it is impossible, for most of us, to have a good life. It is hard to be sure. It is so hard to be sure, that I feel only a saint has the right to refuse; and because of this, I have decided to compromise, and to take up Red Cross work. I cannot feel a hero or a martyr, but only very humble and uncertain. If this were the Kingdom of Heaven, it would be so easy to decide. But is one justified in trying to live as though it were? Are we pacifists on the 'threshold of immorality', as the Master so confidently asserts, or is it the way of life, the 'pearl of great price', that is worth everything else?'.

A day or two later, I met the Archbishop of York. He, and the Master of Balliol were the two Christian thinkers whom

I chiefly admired. Both appreciated the dilemma of the pacifists – both had a deep understanding of the way of Jesus, and of the 'Word made Flesh' in the realities of politics and economics; and both came to the opposite conclusion to that which I had chosen.

My meeting with the Archbishop, William Temple, was brought about by his nephew, Freddy Temple, who was one of my contemporaries at Balliol, and who had decided, as I had, to be a pacifist. Freddy was attracted to the view of 'the Uncle', as we came to call the Archbishop, that pacifism is a call to certain people, 'That is terrifying and stimulating', Freddy wrote to me at the beginning of the war. 'One's belief is so arrogant, that one must be incredibly humble.' He then reminded me of the Master saying that one must be 'perpetually dying', but went on to ask 'Doesn't the Master's and the Uncle's view involve too great an identification of Church and State, . . . the blunder of the church, since Constantine? After the war the Church of England must be disestablished and reformed. And there has to be a federal union of Europe.'

PART 2

WAR WITH THE QUAKERS
AND WAR WITH ARMY

I am recounting in detail the two 'opposite' situations in which I found myself during the Second World War, because the questions they pose lie at the centre of this book. There was intense despair and hope, cruelty and compassion, love and hate, death and life, wherever we looked. Our minds were severed by conflicting emotions as we struggled with what each day and night brought with it, whether we were soldiers or pacifists.

Ever since I was a boy, I had been asking if a soldier would be able to follow the way of Christ. My family had been deeply embroiled in fighting over the centuries. Sir Edmund Verney had been Standard Bearer to the King in the Battle of Edgehill, and refused to surrender the Standard, saying, 'My life is my own, but the Standard is The King's'. He was cut down, and his hand, with its signet ring, was brought back to Claydon House, my family home. He was the family hero, which I and my four brothers felt we had to live up to.

And so, where did that leave me? I was already steeped in stories about the way of Christ, and felt that it was the only way I could go. I hated the shooting of animals on our estate and yet ended my time in the war with a licence to kill and a cocked pistol in my pocket, next to my bible.

'Living with opposites' was hugely accentuated for me during my time in The Cretan Resistance, by agonising doubts, fears and despair. It was the brave Cretan boy who met me by shining his torch on a cliff, when I was first shipped into occupied Crete, that showed me what I was looking for. But that happened 50 years later, when he was dying of cancer in Athens.

The Imperial War Museum have digitalised Stephen Verney's audio tapes of his time in World War II.

WAR WITH THE QUAKERS
IN FINLAND AND NORWAY

᪉᪂᪉

Freddy Temple and I decided we would volunteer for ambulance work and we were both attracted to the idea of working with the Quakers.

'Quakers' was their nickname; their founder, George Fox, had exhorted them to 'tremble' at the word of God. The name which they gave to themselves was The Society of Friends; and the two marks of the Quaker movement which had become generally recognised, were their refusal to take part in a secular war, and their pattern of silent worship.

Freddy and I went to visit Paul Cadbury, a member of one of the great Quaker families. He was in the process of recon-stituting the Friends Ambulance Unit, which had served during the First World War. We were both accepted, and asked to appear in Birmingham on November 15th, at the second training camp. So began for me three and a half years of service with the Quakers.

From them I received new glimpses of 'the glory of God'. The first, which began immediately, was through their pattern of silent worship. Every day, there were intervals when we stopped talking, and sat together in silence. This, to an Anglican, was a new experience, and opened up new dimensions of prayer. Or rather, I should say, a new under-standing of the presence of God; and in particular, of that saying of Jesus 'The kingdom of heaven is within you' [Luke 17.21]. In the original Greek, this saying has a double meaning which holds together the differences between 'within us' and 'amongst us'. The mystery of God involves not only knowing *about* it, but also *knowing it as present in the to and fro between us,* often as we sit in shared silence.

This was the foundation secret of the Society of Friends, the secret of the 'divine light of Christ in every man and woman', which could make us one with each other, in the peace of God.

The profound meaning of the name The Society of Friends became clearer two months later as we went into action. These were the months of what was later to be called 'the phoney war', before the full German attack was launched against the armies of France and Great Britain. But meanwhile another war front was developing. Stalin took the opportunity, while the Allies were fully occupied, to invade Finland, and the huge Russian army was able to overwhelm the tiny Finnish forces. Great Britain was unable, according to Chamberlain's calculations, to go to their aid, though a friend of mine at Balliol – Teddy Heath, who later became Prime Minister, wrote to me from USA, after hearing about the peace terms imposed on Finland, 'No one could be but glad that Finland is spared further slaughter, for the moment, at least, even though it is in many ways a defeat for us as well as for her. But when I read of what the peace means in ordinary human terms – the refugees, the misery and grief – the new lives to be begun – then I feel as I did over Czechoslovakia, and after spluttering incoherently with rage, I relapse into exasperated, because impotent, silence'.

Great Britain could not officially send troops to Finland, but they could allow a private charity, such as the Friends Ambulance Unit to send a unit at their own expense. This is what the Quakers did. We were divided into two parties; the first party arrived in Finland before the war finished; Freddy

Temple and I were chosen to be in the second party which left London, driving our convoy of white ambulances, in the middle of February 1940.

It was on this drive up to Newcastle that I became aware of the wider Society of Friends, of which we were a part. On the first evening we reached Doncaster, and carried our stretchers and sleeping bags into the Friends Meeting house. After a good high tea we went out to explore the town, with orders to be back at 9 pm to meet Doncaster Friends, who were providing refreshments. We grumbled at the prospect of making polite conversation, after a gruelling day, but the event put us to shame. They had prepared, with loving care, a room with a fire and a ring of arm chairs, and we sat round in our slippers, while they plied us with coffee and chocolate biscuits and fruits. Very dignified, elderly men and women they were, and when we were finished, they made little speeches of welcome and good wishes; and Mrs Proctor, who had risen from a sick bed to work and wash up for us, said very simply that she had done it, not in her own name, but in the name of him who died for us all.

On the second night we stayed at Ampleforth, and on the third, at Darlington, where we were given meat pies, and for each of us, a copy of St John's gospel. From these meetings I realised more deeply the reality of that name, 'The Society of Friends'. They are naturally and immediately like life-long friends, not with any display of ostentatious hospitality, but by sympathy and loving kindness.

When we arrived in Newcastle we found that our boat was delayed for at least some days. So Freddy got in touch with 'the uncle' at York, and we were invited to spend a couple of nights with him and his wife. They had no children, and Freddy was regarded as a son. When we arrived, the Arch-

29

bishop was out giving five talks in Bridlington. He leads an almost impossibly busy life. But he gave up much of the next two evenings to being with us. He encouraged us to read the Master of Balliol's new book, 'The Two Moralities', which he had chosen as his Lent book, and which deals with the question of how Love can be reconciled with Justice – the general problem within which pacifism is a particular issue. He also let us have the proofs of his coming publication, 'Thoughts in Wartime'.

These two books, by the thinkers whom I most admired, both said that in this present moment of war, our duty was to fight against Hitler and his Nazis. 'War is a monstrous evil, and killing is bad', writes The Archbishop, 'but it can become an expression of love when every alternative was worse. The mere refusal to fight is a very slender witness to the supremacy of love. That witness seems to require the contracting out, so far as may be, from the advantages as from the obligations of the secular order of society. For example, to live in poverty, with the very poor, and to share their lot, and thereby bring them new strength and hope. The soldier who accepts the call of his duty and performs it with no hatred in his heart, is also showing the way to permeate the world itself with the Christian spirit. The Kingdom of God uses the service of both the Good Samaritan and the Good Centurion'.

The most delightful memory of that visit is of our conversations with 'the uncle' himself, and of how he was hardly ever serious for more than two minutes together, Through those two evenings which he gave up to us, he told us many stories, each witty or uproariously funny. We finished, last thing at night, by saying Compline, the Archbishop reading, and Freddy and I giving the responses.

These two encounters, with The Friends and The Archbishop, were in sharp contrast, The Friends dedicated to pacifism, and The Archbishop believing in the possibility of a just war. They were very different in personality, The Friends with their seriousness and their concerns, The Archbishop with his theology and his ebullient humour. *But they were held together by their personal loyalty to Jesus Christ, in whom those opposites coincided.*

When we got back to Newcastle our boat was still delayed, but a few days later she arrived and we went aboard. I wrote in my diary, 'The convoy formed up, consisting of about 40 ships, without reckoning the destroyers, which were too elusive to count, darting and bouncing around us like dogs out for a walk. Planes kept watch overhead, and a phantom ship which must have been a cruiser, haunted the outskirts of the convoy. There is something to be said for Britain's armed might! We lie down at night fully dressed, and with our life belts ready. Sometimes you don't get more than two minutes after you've hit your mine',

'The greatest pleasure, as we left behind English rationing, was the food in our Norwegian ship. On the first day we had goat's milk cheese and butter *ad libitum,* or as some were to discover, *ad nauseum.* Sailing northward up the Northumberland coast, we turned various hues of green, yellow and white, and as the boat soared and plunged, we groaned, vomited or prayed for torpedoes!'

But our crossing to Oslo passed without accident. There was little talk on board except of the Russian – Finnish negotiations. It was a hard peace, but the alternative was for Finland to become a second Flanders, with the likelihood that the whole of Scandinavia would be involved. I had a conversation with a Belgian officer on board. 'Hitler is a fat pig, a dirty boy', he said; 'and of the salles Russes, to kill, it is my desire, kill, kill, kill, kill, kill, and then [pointing to his forehead] I put my revolver here, tiens! It is finished.'

In contrast, I discovered in Oslo that many Norwegians seemed to be interested in Federal Union. From Oslo we drove along icy roads to Stockholm, where we met one of our first party who had arrived in Finland two or three weeks before the end of the war. He brought back highly coloured tales ... 'Our men spent the first few days lying in a ditch with bombs raining round them. The result was that they all succumbed to acute diarrhoea, and could do nothing in the peaceful intervals but repair the ravages. Two who went up first to the front line had to dress a Finn with bullets whistling past on both sides. They were rigid with fright, and their bowels dribbled. We had had a lecture on hysteria before we left England, and these are, apparently, common symptoms for the first time under fire. Their constant trial had been driving in the dark without headlamps, along unknown roads that were sheets of ice. The question was not whether you went into a ditch, but how many times you went into the ditch. Another danger was the Finns themselves. Some who had sat behind machine guns week after week, mowing down fields of Russians, went mad, as they sat. Others were nervously exhausted, and would shoot if you walked a few yards from where you were working'.

But in spite of the end of their war, the Finns encouraged us to come, and told us that there was more work than ever to be done. We had hoped to be able to drive across the frozen sea – the Gulf of Bothnia – but the spring thaw had begun, and it would not be safe. We had, instead, to drive north to Haparanda, and into the Arctic Circle, and so into

32

Finland. The cold was so intense that if one's naked hand touched metal, the skin stuck. On March 25th we crossed in to Finland. From now on we ate Finnish army rations, which consisted largely of bean soup and black bread. We made our way to Joensuu, which was to be our headquarters, and from which we would evacuate refugees. We were lodged in Swedish army tents. I wrote in my letter home on April 7th, 'the centre pole is a chimney, and at the bottom of it, a wood stove, which we keep burning night and day. We sit up for an hour each, every night, stoking. Last night I stoked from 3 to 4; the man before me let the thing nearly out, and when I took over, the whole tent was muttering and cursing and pulling sleeping bags and blankets round them. By the time I gave over, I had the iron of the stove red hot and the other men were sleeping soundly. We are ten to a tent, but so far, we have not had time to get on each other's nerves. We are transporting convalescents and civilians from Joensuu to Kuopio. We run a regular daily bus service of 6 ambulances along the nightmare 90 miles over frozen ruts. Humphrey Waterfield [my fellow driver] and I, leave tonight at 5 o'clock with the last bus to Kuopio. We should be there by midnight, though if we ditch alone in the dark with a load of women and children, heaven help us.'

In my next letter home dated April 14th, I am already referring to the German invasion of Norway, and the arrival of a British expeditionary force. 'In three days, I shall be coming of age. It is exciting to reach manhood in the heart of a war zone with your line of retreat cut off. You can guess what our plans might be!'. In fact, we were already packing up to leave Finland and make for Norway. We were sad to say goodbye to the Finns. 'They are a very lofty people; passionate, capable of cruelty but full of dignity. They have a wonderful sense of humour, the women are quiet, often beautiful, and always hard working. They accept their defeat realistically; but not as final, for they despise the Russians and are proudly race conscious. All go out of their way to be good to us, and I think we are leaving behind a good will.'

The next letter is dated April 28th, and written from the Swedish-Norweigan frontier. We were waiting for the road over the pass to be repaired by a special squad of Swedes. It can only be crossed at night when it is frozen, for by day it is deep in slush. 'In comparison to this road, we are told, Finland was a picnic. Small cars have to lay bushes under their wheels, and go forward a few yards at a time. Lorries just stick. I wish I could tell you what we shall find on the other side. The dominant factor is the German air-force, whose bombing is ruthlessly thorough and accurate. So far, they have respected the Red Cross. There is practically no food to be had, so we have loaded one of the ambulances with flour. Meanwhile we are eating huge Swedish meals, milk, butter, fruit, eggs, vegetables; all the things we have done without for so long, and that we may not see again. Sweden is wallowing in prosperity; but she is resigned to an inevitable invasion. The prospect of Norway tomorrow with her snow-capped mountains and her blonde maidens, fills me with exhilaration'.

My final letter was written, 'Off the west coast of Scotland' on May 6th, 'Only a very bold submarine could prevent us getting home now. But I shall write down the history of the last week, so that I may remember what really happened'.

Everybody advised us against trying to cross that pass. Even if we did get through, we should have shaken our ambulances to pieces. But we put chains on, improvised guards for the petrol taps, and set off at midnight. By 8.30

the next morning we hadn't reached the pass. The ruts were deeper than in Finland, and we lost several petrol taps. We gave up the attempt for the time being, for the sun was now hot and the pass would be thawed for the day. We pulled up by the roadside to get some sleep. I erected a stretcher on one side of the ambulance, changed into pyjamas, and began to make up for the lost night. After two hours an excited conversation broke into my dreams, something about German planes and machine guns. Humphrey came hurrying up and told me that we had been attacked. I was to get out at once into the forest. 'Someone has been pulling your leg' I replied. A few minutes later, I was positively ordered out of the ambulance [a thing almost unheard of in the FAU.] I was not convinced until I saw the bullet holes. Then I made off hastily into the forest. Two planes had flown down the road and gunned the convoy as far as the Ambulance immediately in front of ours. Had they respected the Red Cross? We guessed that they had only seen it when their fingers were already on the trigger. But the further question arose ... should we go on? A call came through urging us not to. Why not? Our two officers went on in the staff car to try and find out. On their return, they ordered us forward, and issued white camouflage coats.

We started at 9.30 pm, and reached Godjord at 8.30 am, thus covering the 23 miles at an average of 2 mph. The little cars had to be dug out two or three times about every 100 yards; and as we climbed down the mountain into Norway, the snow gave place to mud. Nobody was ashamed to admit that he was exhausted. We dug and shoved while faces grew grey in the morning light, the second morning without sleep.

I remember Freddy without his laugh; David's huge frame drooping over the wheel; Stanley without his dash; Sam looking as though he was giving up the ghost; Brandon unable to tell his right hand from his left. But nobody grew irritable, and there was a sense of triumph that we had achieved what everyone had called impossible. At one point, a German plane made straight toward us, but it seemed to be only a courtesy visit; we were unmolested for the rest of our stay, and we concluded that the Red Crosses were respected.

Meanwhile, our officers reported to Colonel Beveridge, the CO of The Medical Corps. By his uneasiness he gave them the impression that an evacuation was contemplated, but he made arrangements with them to distribute our ambulances among the British, French and Norwegian troops. Those of us in the British contingent went forward along an unspeakable road towards Namsos. We were met by an officer who drove up and said that he did not wish to be inhospitable, but there would be a lot of movement on that road tonight, and 'it would be in the interests of democracy and all that' if we turned back. It was an odd message. Richard, our commandant was disturbed, so he and Humphrey went off to Namsos in the staff car, and learnt that there was indeed to be an evacuation or a retreat tonight. General Carton de Wyat had been ever so sorry that no arrangements had been made for us. He advised us to drive back into Sweden, and was really full of apologies. On their way back, Richard and Humphrey came to the conclusion that we should be worse than useless in Sweden, even if we got there, for we had no petrol. It was decided that Humphrey and I were to drive to Namsos to ask General Carton de Wyat [who is reported to have one eye, one lung and one leg] whether he could find room for us on board. Three ambulances were to follow and bring all our kit down to a specified place near Namsos quai.

The road to Namsos had, earlier, been full of marching troops and packed lorries. Now, it was deserted. Huge trucks were driven deliberately into the ditch, and the whole route was lined with the casts off of the retreating army. We were the last British to cross that road; we were behind the rearguard of a retreating army – fortunately, for our peace of mind, we did not know it.

When we reached Headquarters, we were set quite at ease. Only two officers were left. One, a colonel, and the other, presumably, his adjutant. We drove up at high speed, and as I jumped out, I knocked the door of our staff car against the back of an old broken backed Ford. 'Hello!', said the adjutant. 'What do you want? You know, old man, you must be careful of our car. It's valuable.' They were both taking the air, smoking as though after an excellent dinner, 'By all means. Plenty of room for you on board. Only two of you? 53 chaps? Yes we can fit them in', Not a hair was out of place. 'You've plenty of time. We shan't be off before four. Probably we won't all get away tonight'. We arranged to meet them on their way into Namsos, and to follow them down to the quai.

We found our FAU friends at the rendezvous, wedged into three ambulances, with their pockets full of bully beef and biscuits. A few minutes later, the remnant of the general staff drove up. They gave the prearranged signal, and we drew in behind them.

Namsos was in ruins, lit by fires from the ammunition dumps. A few pillars, still upright, stood sentinel over what had been a town, and was now a twisted, charred wilderness. The pale faces of the marching troops mingled with the flickering fires, and there was a shuddering sense of the triumph of evil. We drove our little white convoy down to the quay, and then crashed everything into the debris, and left them. Later they were burnt and blown up with the quay itself. It is difficult to go on writing – perhaps those Red Crosses, like their prototype, will have their Easter. It is hard to see that we did anything to justify carrying them.

But then there was no time for thought. Staff officers with red bands hurried up. 'Who are you?'.

'British Red Cross'.

'This way, hurry along.' We hurried.

By the light of a huge bonfire, streams of khaki clad figures were pouring into the side of a monstrous grey hull. We followed into her murky interior. She was – I believe, a pleasure cruiser that toured between France, Spain and Morocco, named the *El Djezair*. That night, she packed into her holds 11,000 British troops, some 200 Frenchmen and about 50 sick. I got floor space outside an ex-dining room on a landing. This was after I had been turned off the floor of his cabin by a fat officer with little to be said in his favour. Tommies flopped down all round. Some had been marching for days on end, and all were utterly exhausted. They had lost all their personal kit and most of their military equipment. From the day they landed in Norway, it had been a succession of disasters. They were chivvied continuously by the German air-force, against which they could put up no sort of resistance. Three quarters of their stores had been destroyed, as they were landed. A lot of their guns had not landed. They retreated from one untenable position to another, short of food, short of sleep, doing forced marches to avoid capture. How the staff organised the evacuation as efficiently as they did remains a matter for amazement. And the spirit of the troops was magnificent; there was no straggling and no complaining.

We sailed about two o'clock, as another day dawned on Namsos Fjord. Two troop ships, with a strong escort of destroyers and cruisers, and not a German plane in sight. I went in, and lay for some hours shivering on top of an assortment of rifles, bren guns, gas masks and haversacks, with the limbs of various soldiers twisted amongst them.

Later in the morning, there was a sudden explosion, and the ship's engines seemed to stop. 'Torpedoed' was the obvious reaction, and the whole floor rose together and made for the deck. But almost before we had moved, there was another explosion, and then another, and it was recognised as gunfire. The Germans had learnt of our departure, and were giving us a good send off.

The attack continued off and on for about three hours. It was a glorious May morning, with sunshine on a blue sparkling sea, and I stood on deck and watched what must have been, so far, one of the biggest sea fights of the war. The planes came over in waves; at one point I counted six, and they seemed to attack one ship at a time. They dived vertically, one behind the other, released each one a salvo of bombs, and made off. The ships replied with blazing anti aircraft guns; they seemed to stand up on their haunches and spit like furious cats. We must have been attacked first, and bombs fell close in the water. Two of our ships were reported hit, and five planes were brought down.

I felt myself to be a spectator, and not a participant in this action. As such, I could appreciate the glamour of war; it was a game where men played for their lives. One side had mastery of the sea, one of the air, and from their respective elements, they thundered up and down at one another with their batteries of destruction. War is very heroic for the spectator.

Meanwhile, on board the *El Djezair,* we were seeing another side of the picture. The men had with them one day's rations of bully beef and biscuits. Beside this, the French had a limited supply of water, an even more limited supply of *vin ordinaire,* and a few potatoes and beans. The food was issued at irregular intervals, and the men lined up for it in two long queues. Each carried his own billy-can in which a quantity of whatever had been slopped out might be conveyed safely to the deck. The French [as we imagined, in our need to blame somebody] had no ideas of cleanliness or order, and the result was rude chaos. The lavatories became choked, so that the men who had been sleeping in them moved out into the already overcrowded corridors. Few had room even to stretch themselves out straight. Water for washing was turned off, except for a few isolated and unpredictable hours. In the midst of this disorder, we managed to keep our identity as a unit. Paul did some smart work in the kitchen, and brought up food for 25, which we ate on the port deck from the few billy-cans we had salvaged. Walter did valiant deeds in the hold, with sticking plaster and lint, for most of the men had cuts and sores.

We reached Scapa Flow on Sunday morning at 4 am, after 50 hours at sea. The oddest sensation was to see a green field! No meals were served that morning or afternoon, but at about 3 pm, we were transferred to the *Reina del Pacifico,* a British boat that cruises, in peace time, round South America. As we came on board, we were given a mug of hot, sweet tea. The FAU were the last to get on board, and the men's quarters were already full, so we were led by a white coated steward, through the sergeants' mess and shown into third class cabins. There were white sheets on the bunks, a mirror, hanging cupboards and running water.

I nearly burst into tears. The best I had hoped for was a space on the floor to stretch myself out; but here was cleanliness and plenty of room to recover one's own personality. Food too, lots of it, and served at tables on plates, And a hot salt water bath.

When we disembarked at Glasgow, we were lined up to hear a short speech of welcome given by a Field Marshal from the War Office. 'Remember this', he said, 'you were not driven out of Norway. You were ordered out'.

WAR WITH THE QUAKERS
IN GLOUCESTER

ξ➤◄ξ

Hardly had we landed when the phoney war turned into the hot war. Hitler invaded Belgium and the Netherlands. Chamberlain resigned on May 10th 1940. Churchill became the leader of a National Government.

Meanwhile, we had gone home for a short rest. I wrote to Freddy, who was with his mother and his sister, Ann, 'When Ann chivvies you out of the bath, remember, you were not driven out, you were ordered out'.

Two weeks later, he let me know that he was being sent to 'a frightful hospital in Gloucester'. These were the days of the evacuation from Dunkirk, when 335,000 British and French troops were cut off by the Germans, and brought across the channel in a fleet of little boats. Many needed hospital care, and one of the Emergency Hospitals made ready for them was the City General Hospital in Gloucester. There I joined Freddy and a group of FAU men, to work as orderlies and porters.

We slept on the floor of the Friends Meeting House, and worked a 54 hour week, as well as getting up at night if there was an air-raid alarm. We were given the most sordid jobs, like sorting out the rubbish in the dust-bins. At first the hospital staff viewed us with hostility, but they quickly discovered that we were willing and efficient. However, Councillor Lear of the City Council moved a motion launching an attack on 'conchies in funk holes'. He spoke of the men fighting for King and country, and how we were devouring the rates paid by their nearest and dearest in the City of Gloucester. The Mayor then rose, and drew the attention of the City Council to Standing Order 92 Section b, which gives the Mayor power to bring any discussion to a close. He made an eloquent speech, proving how courageous we all were – the nephew of The Archbishop, for example, who had incurred social ostracism. He quoted the Dean of The Cathedral saying that it would be a blot on the fair name of Gloucester if we were dismissed, and finished with a peroration about Christianity. The Chairman of The Medical Committee seconded, and it was put to the vote. We had a majority of 16 to 13. Councillor Lear rose and said, 'Good morning, Mr Mayor. This is the dirtiest day's work you have ever done'. He returned to the attack later, but was never quite able to overturn our majority.

By this time Freddy had been 'promoted'; he had gone to London as a Group Leader, with the job of visiting and encouraging the local units, and I had taken his place as a leader of the Gloucester section. We continued with our hard and menial work as orderlies and porters, but we had now moved into three slum cottages, where we could begin to build up our own community life. It began to appear to us that if we were to give a true pacifist witness, we had to do more than show the world how brave we were. We had to become a *Christian Community,* to work out together how people could live in the spirit of Christ, and so hope to do something to remove the occasion for war. This is the Quaker peace testimony.

But what did that way demand of us in wartime? While we were being tossed by storms in our Quaker teacup, the war was growing fiercely around us. Coventry was bombed, and the Cathedral reduced to a heap of ruins. The Provost, Dick

Howard, set up a charred cross in the sanctuary where the altar had been, and above it, on a wall, the words 'Father Forgive', the words of Jesus, as he was being crucified. A month later, I went to stay with him and his family, and he took me on a tour of the ruins. I saw some mediaeval nails lying on the floor, and picked up two of them and tied them together into the shape of a cross. Dick Howard told me that this was the origin of the 'Coventry Cross of Nails', which, over the next generation, was sent out all over the world as a sign of reconciliation. [Later it transpires that mine may not have been the first; a Coventry vicar, whose church had suffered grievous damage, had made such a cross on the morning after the air-raid, and taken it to the Bishop. Two of us, and maybe even more, had glimpsed the same vision of glory coming out of suffering.] I carried my Cross of Nails in my rucksack throughout the war, and after the peace, gave it to a German woman who was a minister serving in East Germany behind the iron curtain.

Those bombs which had destroyed Coventry Cathedral, had at the same time blown a hole in the exclusiveness of the Church of England, and brought Christians together in a decision to build, after the war, a Chapel of Unity. I was even beginning to doubt the exclusiveness of Christianity, working as I was in a Unit which included many fine 'agnostics'. I wrote to 'the uncle' at York to ask for his advice. He replied with his accustomed humility on March 17th – 'I was horrified to see that your letter was dated Feb 28th. I do apologise. My secretary has been ill, so that I had to write a lot of my official letters by hand ... Your position is a restatement of Article 13 [among the 39.] If a pious pagan, eg Socrates, acts in accordance with a right conscience, is this action at the command of Christ? It *is* at

44

the command of the Logos – or may be. I always want to start from John 1.9. The Light lightens everyman. Yet, only in the historic Christ does it shine fully. Therefore, only in conscious response to Him can we be sure of walking in the true Light. Elsewhere there is always doubt, and usually some positive error, [a] because of defect in the medium through which the Light reaches us, [b] because of distortion in our own perception or reception of the Light. Do your 'Friends' think they are perfect; if not, how do they propose to advance towards perfection? Is it by the effort of their *ex hypothesi* imperfect wills?

I am afraid this won't help much, but it is the best I can offer.'

For the next 6 months we worked in Gloucester on the task of building a Christian Community. I wrote to my parents, – 'The work we have been doing has grown out of T S Eliot's 'Idea of a Christian Society' [which had recently been published]. You remember his scheme that inside the state there should be a community of Christians who would be the core or mainspring of Christianity, keeping it alive, and trying to guide social and political change in the light of their faith.

For a long time I have felt at Gloucester that there was no use working or thinking unless the work and thought was guided by Christian worship. But there is quite a minority of us here who are definitely not Christian, and a large majority who are only half hearted. So we are trying to start a 'community of Christians' inside the section. It will be nothing organised, nor will it interfere with, or annoy the others.

But I am sure that in some wholehearted fellowship of that sort, meeting together for worship, thinking together and working together will generate a power of the spirit that would be immeasurable. The spirit always seems to work if you give it half a chance, and I don't see why we should not give it a whole chance.

It is a dangerous venture to get this thing going, because one tends, inevitably to become self righteous. But if we can pray as the Publican, 'Have mercy on me, the sinner', all should be well. I have realised recently, that hitherto, I have been a Pharisee!'

Looking back, 50 years later, I believe now that in Gloucester we were being allowed a glimpse of the back of the mystery of Love, as we tried to hold together the opposites, and celebrate *unity* in *diversity*.

As the spring turned into summer, the war became more frenzied. On April 27th 1941 the Germans captured Athens, and on May 20th invaded Crete. I became more and more doubtful about my pacifism, and wrote to Freddy ' The future is very uncertain. Perhaps in the next few months, the war will be over and the Germans in London. Perhaps we shall be with the FAU in Greece or Turkey. Perhaps I shall be in the RAF'. Meanwhile Freddy became more and more convinced that pacifism was his vocation. The immediate solution for both of us came in June, when the FAU decided to send a second contingent out to Syria, to work with the Free French. Freddy was to be in charge of this group, and I was invited to join it. We embarked on July 23rd, carrying books to brush up our French, and to start learning Arabic.

WAR WITH THE QUAKERS
IN THE MIDDLE EAST

༄༅

Once again we were aboard a troopship, living with the British Army and with a contingent of Free French. I wrote to my parents, ' The French are a charming lot, and have the atmosphere of volunteers. They must be men of forceful character to have made the choice to go on fighting under de Gaulle. They treat us with the greatest kindness and respect. The British, on the other hand, are puzzled by 'these conscientious objectors'. I overheard them talking in the galley – 'Who are these fuckers?'. 'They're fucking objectives'. Their use of language did not necessarily imply hostility, they were using the words available to them. But the French talk about the same subject with such a wealth of vocabulary and such liveliness of imagination, that it is a continual delight to listen'.

We organised a course of study to prepare us for our future work – French, Medicine and Mechanics. Freddy and I and two others embarked on Arabic. I was looking forward to a time of uninterrupted study, rather like Oxford, but my dream was disrupted by my decision to start a Male Voice Choir on board. We started it with FAU members and one officer, but we were quickly joined by many of the soldiers; we sang for Sunday Services, and took part in Ship's concerts. I'm afraid I used to bully my choir into attending rehearsals even when the sea was rough, and one of the army officers, a splendid Scot, took his revenge one Sunday morning by preaching a sermon on pacifism. He said that he

47

would always put the worship of God in the forefront of the ship's duties, and he preached with wisdom and humility out of a quite first class mind. He ended his sermon by attacking pacifism, showing that there was another genuine Christian way of resisting evil.

On September 23rd we arrived in Beirut to begin our work – taking food and medicines to remote villages. We were wonderfully welcomed by American families, associated with the University, and in particular by the Leavitts, a golden family who provided me with a home from home. Leslie and Margaret, the parents, preserved my sanity, listened to my doubts, and offered total hospitality. They had two sons at college in USA, and two teenage daughters, Marga and Helen, with whom we all fell in love.

But as 1942 began, the war was entering a more dangerous phase for England. A German army was advancing on Egypt along the North African coast, and in the Far East the two Battleships, HMS Repulse and Prince of Wales were sunk by Japanese aircraft. Our little Ambulance Unit was ordered to go to help in the battle of Libya. We camped in the Libyan Desert, and on February 16th, we heard Churchill on the radio; 'I speak to you', he said, 'under the shadow of a great Imperial Disaster; Singapore has fallen'. He made it sound like a great moment of history, in which we should all be proud to share.

I was put in charge of a ward of British soldiers, in a huge casualty clearing station on the outskirts of Tobruk. The waste and desolation of the Libyan Desert struck deep into my soul. Our own medical services were hopelessly over-whelmed by the flood of casualties which was pouring into the hospital from the battle with the Germans which was going on only 20 miles away. My ward was filled with the less seriously wounded, and with those who were suffering from shell shock and psychological breakdowns. There were 85 beds and most of the patients had dysentery. One single orderly had been working there twelve hours a day. Only one window was open, the others were all blacked out; the floor was caked in sand and heaps of tins and cigarette ends; empty boxes and stacks of paper lay piled around. A few bottles of medicine stood on a table, covered by a filthy sheet. A black towel hung over a derelict washbasin. The bed pans were full of faeces that had stood till they were hard, on top of which the patients deposited their new excreta. The patients themselves lay in the semi darkness on stretchers with dirty, bloodstained blankets; they were booked in, fed, and booked out again when a hospital ship managed to reach the harbour. Any kind of treatment went by the board. Nobody was to blame. The orderly had done heroic work but an air of despondency hung heavily around us.

Fortunately, there were now two people from the Friends' Ambulance Unit, myself and one other. We opened the windows and made the sick men more comfortable. We swept the floor, arranged the patients' kit, cleaned the bedpans, gave out medicines, got a clean towel for the basin, and found a piece of soap. Men kept coming in, and by the evening of the second day, with the hospital ship due next morning, we had stretchers on every square foot of floor, but the ward reasonably in hand. I had an evening which became one of those rare and wonderful moments which is as fresh today as it was then – it was an evening when I made a round, after dark, giving out what medicines I had, but more important, talking to each man, exchanging news, finding cigarettes, trying to soothe the shell-shocked, and generally trying to make them all feel that they needn't worry any more, that each of them was a personality that mattered, and had relatives, and a home, and the dignity of being human, and a life that would be worth taking up again. For one of those rare moments, I forgot myself and was happy. And in that ward, that evening, despair was transformed into compassion. My egocentricity had taken a back seat. I was not a superior person doing 'good'. We were all in it together and felt close to each other. Love had broken through all barriers, and Glory shone through.

By now, the war in Libya seemed to have reached a standstill and the immediate prospect of being taken prisoner had given way to thoughts of an advance. A new opportunity opened up for me – Michael Rowntree, from one of the great Quaker families, suggested that Leslie Butler and I should go back to Syria, to open up clinics in the Arab villages. The two of us were sent to the river Khabur region in Northern Syria, where the modern Iran meets the modern Iraq, on the border of Turkey. We were accompanied by an Armenian doctor called Emman Shirajian. The river Khabur is mentioned in the bible as the place where the prophet Ezekiel was ' among the captives' [the refugees], and where 'the hand of the Lord was upon him'. In his day, those refugees were Jews, dumped there by the Babylonians, and in my day, they were Assyrians, a Christian minority who had fled from Turkey during the First World War, under threat of genocide.

These Assyrians still speak Syriac, the language of Jesus. Their settlement is spread over 20 miles, along the banks of the river, and their houses are built of mud and straw in the shape of beehives. They had built a hospital of 17 beehives, but hitherto there were no doctors or nurses to serve there, and the outlying villages were far away.

War with the Quakers in the Middle East

We began by sleeping in the hospital, and sallying forth each day to a different village. Our doctor Emman Shirajian was trained at the American University in Beirut. He was 31, very modest and cheerful, and a good musician; he had brought his violin with him, and we sang together in harmony. He was one of the most brilliant doctors in the Middle East, and as the nearest hospital was 100 miles away across the desert, he was willing to undertake surgery where necessary. Leslie Butler acted as his assistant, sterilising instruments, taking the particulars of patients, doing dressings and assisting with operations. After a while, Leslie was replaced by my old friend Freddy Temple, who, like me, had no great experience of science, surgery or medicines. I myself had to visit the local potentates and was in charge of finance; but my chief work was as dispensing chemist and anaesthetist. Luckily, for both me and Freddy, and indeed the patients, the doctor was a good teacher.

Before long, I was dispensing drugs to some 8,000 souls with a little pair of scales, and a cracked measuring glass. I wrote to my parents, 'We start the week on a Monday with two villages at the lower end of the settlement, one in the morning and one in the afternoon. The local Headman, or Muchta, rigs up a curtain in the village schoolroom, behind which the doctor and Freddy disappear. I take up my stand in front of the curtain, and range my bottles, pills and ointments on a table. Meanwhile Freddy is trying to decide, through an interpreter, who are the most seriously sick cases. The whole population seems to be there – old men on crutches, old women with gaunt faces, big fat neurotic women, mothers and children, the local priest with eye trouble and a lot of small boys who fetch me water or act as policemen in controlling the mob. At first, we let everybody

51

into the room, but the noise and heat and crowding was intolerable. Last week they surged towards me, and knocked over my bottles, so we now keep everyone firmly outside.

Gradually the patients emerge from behind the curtain with a paper, on which is written their name, diagnosis and treatment. Then, the exhausting procedure of giving the prescribed medicine. I begin by insisting that they bring their own bottle, so they tramp off home to get one. Then, the instructions – 3 times a day after meals. The patient looks puzzled. Before or after meals? After. Twice a day? No, three times. Three times a day before meals? . . . So it goes on for three hours, till some 25 or 30 patients have been treated. But do they take the medicine? I was called, one day by the government representative in the central village to tell me that he had been to many doctors, but none of them had healed him. He opened a cupboard and showed me all the medicines that had been prescribed, none of which had actually been swallowed.

It is impossible to treat everybody in our little clinic, and mothers get desperate as we start packing up to leave. It is heart breaking. But we have worked to the limit of our endurance and beyond that of the doctor'.

As I mentioned earlier, my other 'chief work' was as an anaesthetist, when the doctor was performing operations in one of our little beehives. What stands out in my mind during this period was an incident when I almost killed one of my patients by administering an overdose of chloroform. The doctor had taught me that anaesthetists usually started with chloroform until the patient stopped coughing and was well and truly 'under'. Then came ether. One day we had to operate on a middle aged man with a strangulated hernia. I kept on with the chloroform because this man would not stop coughing. Suddenly the doctor shouted 'My God, his blood's gone black!' We took off the mask and tried to resuscitate him but nothing worked, not even an injection into his heart. As a last resort, the doctor took a blunt instrument and pushed it up the patient's backside. The man let out a loud 'Ugh' and [thankfully] started to breathe again. I told this story many years later at a dinner for anaesthetists, and they assured me that the blunt instrument treatment was, in fact, recommended for use in extreme crises. Even today, I tremble at the thought of being so close to killing another human being, not with a bomb or a gun, but by my own clumsiness and insensitivity.

But in spite of our failings, Freddy and I persevered under the watchful eye of our magnificent doctor, and later in life, when we were both Bishops in the Church of England, we would remember with trepidation the administering of the medicines, but recall with joy our numerous cataract operations, and restoring sight to so many of the Assyrians who had entrusted themselves to us.

By the second winter, our hospital was functioning, and patients were being admitted for days and nights. But how were we to keep them warm? Who would give us wood? I had tried various people, without success, and I was becoming desperate.

Finally, I went to the Mayor of our local town, and during our conversation, it became obvious that if I gave him a bribe – a sweetener – I would get the wood, and if I did not give the bribe and embrace 'corruption', I would not get the wood. There had been other incidents when rich merchants from Aleppo had used our hospital facilities, and then refused to pay, but this wood incident was the straw that broke the camel's back. I decided that I had to resign from the Friends' Ambulance Unit. I had, finally, woken to the reality of corruption in the world.

REFLECTION ON MY TIME WITH
THE QUAKERS

I wrote to my parents in 1943 saying 'I have been utterly wrong, and wrong for the worse possible reasons'.

Fifty five years later, I can see, in retrospect, the truth in that judgement. My reasons for being a pacifist were wrong, and my reasons for resigning from the Friends' Ambulance Unit were also wrong.

I was a pacifist because of the wrong idea of God. I thought of Him as a benign person who never got angry or punished us. The world he had created was made in that same image; it was a benign place, where, if only human beings were kind to each other, peace would naturally prevail. That picture did not allow for evil, as in Hitler's Nazi movement, nor for the puzzle of human egocentricity. In the Middle East, I was coming to know a different world, reflecting a different God. I turned to the Old Testament, and began to feel that it was as exciting as a good novel. I became aware that this other God was revealing Himself, but that I hadn't recognised Him in England's green and pleasant land, or in the privileged society in which I had been brought up. But when I met those merchants from Aleppo and those government officials, and then read the words of Amos, written about 750 BC, my eyes were opened to see another aspect of God's character – his Kabod – his weight – his glory.

'Listen to this, you who grind the destitute and plunder the humble. . . . .giving short measure in the bushel and taking over-weight in the silver, tilting the scales fraudulently and selling the dust of the wheat . . . the Lord has sworn: I will never forget any of their doings. The time is coming, says the Lord God, I will smash them all into pieces, and I will kill them to the last man with the sword. No fugitive shall escape, no survivor find safety . . . if they are herded into captivity by their enemies, there will I bid the sword slay them, and I will fix my eye on them for evil and not for good'.

What is the name of the God who issues those awful threats? He told Moses, 'My name is I AM THAT I AM' – or it can also be translated I WILL BE WHAT I WILL BE. In the world that I have created, things are what they are, and will be what they will be. The physical reality he has created for us, in which we can grow up, is governed by stable laws, such as the law of gravity – if we jump out of a window, we shall fall to the ground. Similarly, if we fail to live by the commandment 'Love one another', we shall have to suffer the consequences. Wickedness, though it may appear to prosper in the short term, will, in the end, have to pay a fearful price.

We find it difficult to accept that this god of righteousness can be the same God who is revealed in the compassion of Jesus. But Jesus himself did not find that a problem. He grew up in that harsh world. When he was a few weeks old, his parents became refugees to escape a bloody massacre by a mad old tyrant. As a young man, he was driven by the spirit of God into the desert, where he came to know the reality of good and evil confronting each other in the desert of his own human psyche; and the God of his fathers springing up like a fountain of water, out of the depths of himself. The same God, who had declared his righteousness, now also declared his mercy. In Jesus the opposites coincided, as psalm 85 had foreseen that one day they must do. 'Mercy and truth are met together; righteousness and peace have kissed each other'.

God in eternity does not change his mind, but what he can reveal of Himself, changes in time according to what we are able to ask for and to receive. My reasons for being a pacifist were based on a limited understanding of God; and my reasons for resigning my pacifism were based on an equally limited understanding of human society. Those rich merchants and government officials had not been brought up in a society where they would expect to be approached by a 'charity'. They might have given generously, if they had been called upon to show mercy. But, approached by a member of 'the master race', they naturally expected to bargain.

My condemnation of myself, and that consciousness of being 'utterly wrong' was, as I see in retrospect, a part of the truth, but not the whole of it. The original Quaker experience, in 1646, had been of an anguished searching for truth and, in emptiness, the conviction of sin. 'In this iron furnace I toiled and laboured', wrote one of them. But it led to a transforming consciousness of the divine light within each human soul, and the spirit of Christ dwelling amongst them. Those first Friends, during the English Civil War, had seen the emptiness of the existing churches and of their outward forms. As they longed to know God in their own hearts, and in each other, they were led to worship in small groups where they could meet each other, and in silence, through which God could come to them and speak with them. These Quaker truths are elements of the 'way' which Jesus showed to his first disciples, and which we must rediscover if his spirit is to make his home among us. But they are not the whole way.

George Fox, the founder of the Society of Friends, as he rejected the outward signs of ecclesiastical pomp, had probably not heard of the humble Anglican vicar named George Herbert, who died in 1633, for whom to put on vestments was a deeply spiritual act, a sign of deference to Christ, to cover his own unworthiness. The centre of the truth the Friends were searching for, or that which was searching for them, was not the spiritual emptiness of the churches, but their own spiritual emptiness, through which they would come to know the glory of God. George Fox and George Herbert were both conscious of this. They were spiritual brothers as they followed in the way of Jesus, 'who emptied himself, and became obedient unto death ... wherefore God has highly exalted him' – to become the focus of a new life revealing the glory of God the Father. The way to that glory is through suffering. This was the message of the risen Christ on Easter Day. 'The Son of Man must needs suffer, and so enter into glory'.

He had already warned his disciples, 'narrow is the door, and full of affliction is the way that leads to life, and there are few who find it'. The way is through the letting go of egocentricity. It is the way through the death of 'I' into the life of 'I AM' – the life of God, the Father in his sons and daughters. That way is the truth; and that truth is the life. 'I AM the way, and the truth, and the life', he had said to them.

But nobody can come to know the truth of God, in any of his revelations of Himself unless he has passed through that 'narrow door'; emptiness is the unity we all have to share.

That is the word – the logos – of God which lightens everyman. But those who have passed through the door which is Jesus, have entered into a unity, lived out in diversity. There, George Fox worships God in silence, and George Herbert worships through poetry and music. George Fox rejects sacraments, so that we may not be led astray by signs which we confuse with the reality towards which they point, while George Herbert believes that God is revealed through signs; 'teach me, my God and King, in all things thee to see'. One is not right and the other wrong; if God lives behind the coincidence of opposites, we can only give thanks for both of them, and learn from both of them.

The same is true about pacifism. George Fox teaches his followers to refuse military service, and to follow Jesus in the perfect way of the cross. George Herbert knows that he can't avoid the opposites, but that God holds them together.

> Whether I fly with angels, fall with dust,
> Thy hands made both, and I am there.
> Thy power and love, my love and trust,
> Make one place everywhere.

Those three and a half years with the Quakers were a privilege for me, and chiefly because they showed me the two truths which lie at the heart of their tradition. First, that the way to God's glory is through emptiness, – an emptiness which can be experienced through silent worship; and secondly, that the character of God's glory is unity in diversity which is expressed in their name, 'The Society of Friends'.

These two truths together point towards an answer to what I have called the puzzle of our egocentricity.

Why did God create the human race egocentric? Because, in the first part of our life, we have to develop the strong ego which we will then be able to share with each other. The greatest love, says Jesus, is 'to put your *psyche* for our friends.' This is usually translated as 'to lay down your lives for our friends', which was the climax of the cross towards which Jesus was led by his love. But the Greek words in St John's gospel do not say precisely this, and to translate them in such a way lets us off the hook, for we are not likely to be faced daily with that choice between physical life and death. What Jesus is commanding his disciples to do is something more mundane; it is to put our egocentricity 'for our friends', a choice which confronts us daily, from moment to moment.

Why should God create us with this inbuilt contradiction? With both a strong ego, and a need to let that ego go? Because our true destiny is to love with the love of God; so we shall have to reach that point of emptiness where we cry out for God's mercy, and ask for the gift of his Spirit.

The Quakers hold this emptiness within their tradition. They hold also, implicit in their name, that diversity in unity which points towards the character – the Kabod – of God.

When we use the word 'God', what do we imagine? People often say to me, 'I no longer believe in God'. My usual response is, 'Tell me what you don't believe'. Then after listening, I invariably have to say, 'I don't believe in that kind of 'god' either.

Then I feel able to talk about the Quakers, who recognise God most readily in our relationships with each other. I can tell them too about a Russian Orthodox painter, a saintly man called Rublev, who painted an icon in the 14th century to reveal what God is like. He painted not one figure, but three

– sitting round a table and interacting with each other; and it is *in the relationship between them that we see the glory of God*. Those three are the Father, the Son, and the Holy Spirit; the Father is the Love which is the source of our being, the Son is that Love becoming a human being, and the Holy Spirit is Love holding us together. Their interaction is called the *perichoresis* of the Trinity, where *peri* means 'around', and *choresis* 'giving place to each other'. First the Son and the Spirit give place to the Father, and recognise his authority. But at the same time, the Father and the Spirit give place and all authority to the Son. And finally the Father and the Son give place and all authority to the Spirit, who will become the to and fro of Love between us.

This insight into the nature of God goes back, of course, to the New Testament, to St John who writes that 'God is Love'. When I, myself, was growing up as an Anglican, I found this difficult to understand, and imagined God as a sort of Arch-bishop. The Quakers helped me to return to the true Anglican and Catholic understanding that, in the end, *we cannot imagine God*. We can only say, 'God is Love'; and because Love 'is to put your soul for your friends', then it is something we can't imagine. It is something which we have to *do*.

As I remember my years with the Quakers, I am deeply grateful to them, particularly for highlighting three truths.

First, that God is within each of us, and springs out of the depths of us, like a fountain of water. The Quakers learn this through silence.

Secondly, that God is amongst us. We meet him in our relationships, The Society of Friends has been demonstrating this for over 350 years.

Thirdly, that God cannot be defined in words, or managed in pictures. WE know Him as we *do* the truth of I AM – like the Quakers in South Africa during the apartheid regime, and like the many whom I met in the FAU during the war.

Having paid that tribute, I must also add that the Quakers are not saints. They are flawed human beings, who, like the rest of us, have the opposites of their virtues. Many of them, again like the rest of us, have lost the spontaneity of their founding fathers, and live at second hand by principles. Their society, having rejected the unreality of the churches, has, sadly, at the same time, deprived them of music and the sacraments.

But none of us, and no one church, has been able to reflect the whole glory of God, and we need each other, so that we may let go our own half truths to rediscover the whole truth together – the truth which was held together in Jesus, who was put to death for being anti-establishment, but who told his disciples to keep every detail of the traditional Law, and to teach it to others.

And on Maundy Thursday evening he said to them, 'As you put your *psyche* for each other in my name, my spirit will come, and will guide you into all truth.'

WAR WITH THE ARMY - TRAINING

I took my oath of allegiance to our King and his successors, one morning toward the end of July 1943. The officer in charge of the recruiting station in Cairo said to me, 'This afternoon, you will go down to the Recruits Training Centre on the Suez Canal.'

'I can't possibly do that,' I replied. 'I'll have to spend the rest of today packing up.' 'You're in the army now,' he said, 'but I will give you a day's leave.'

So the next day I went to the Suez Canal, feeling quite frightened, and expecting to be shouted at by NCOs who would batter me into military shape. But I was pleasantly surprised. We were a strangely colourful company of people. The Centre was designed for local recruits, who, having the doubtful privilege of British citizenship, had been called to the colours under a recent order in council. I met 3 Greek speaking Cypriots – one was a cafe proprietor, another was a cook at a big hotel; the third ran what looked like a cigarette store, but he actually made his money out of smuggled whiskey. Then there were Maltese who spoke Italian and French. One of them was a Gymnastic Instructor, a man of magnificent physique, who always needed to be in the limelight. If we are stood at ease for a moment, he starts exercising himself, or breaks into a throaty rendering of 'Sole Mio'. For the first two days he was joking at the pot-bellies of the other recruits; but on the third day, he developed a blister on his toe, and became completely deflated because he could not keep up with the marching.

But the funniest group was a party of rich business men from Alexandria. We called one of them, 'The Informer', because his chief delight was to tell stories about the other three. They were all Cotton Merchants, and one of them, called Kabrit, owned fifteen race horses. They wanted to bring their private cars, but it was forbidden; Kabrit offered the corporal a race horse, but got nowhere. They brought with them a crate of beer, huge boxes of chocolates and all kinds of other delicacies, and each day, they sent out an Arab workman to buy them melons and grapes. Between them they set up an arrangement which must be unique in military history; they employed another recruit from the next tent as a batman. He was called Mohammed Ali, a swarthy Bedouin, who knew a good thing when he saw it. They paid him fantastically – The Informer told us it was 10 shillings a day!. In return, he ran errands, laid out their kit, gathered up everything at night and made the beds; he fetched water, cleaned up around the tent, and washed the billy-cans after meals. When Kabrit was feeling a little seedy, after his injection, he even performed the more unmentionable and unsavoury duties of a hospital orderly. While on these jobs, Mohammed dressed in white underclothes and a white turban, so as to look, as near as possible, like a pukka Sudanese servant. He acted superbly, thus ensuring that the Cotton Merchants maintained their former dignity, as they lay on paliasses in the desert sand, after the exertions of parade.

Then there was Mr Betts, a class conscious accountant who worried about appearing at home 'in these clothes'. He kept up a running fight about social positions with Pantazides, the big fat cook who retaliated by turning up the end of his nose with his podgy hand, and throwing doubt on Mr Betts' manhood.

My family so enjoyed my letters about my new companions, but they were anxious about me and my undecided future in the Army. They urged me to use my Certificate 'A', which I had gained in the Harrow School Officers' Training Corps and to claim that I was, already, a budding officer. But this would have been a farce; what we had learned at school was to present arms, and to form fours, and even that, I had largely avoided by joining the Band. I myself felt glad to be where I was. It had shown me the truth of the line, 'he that is down need fear no fall'. There was a freedom in being a private soldier. The Army can do what it likes to your body; turn it about, march it, make it perform movements with a rifle or a spade or a scrubbing brush. But it can't touch your mind in the same way. My mind lay fallow, and at night it could roam away on the wings of imagining, or turn its energies to study, or lie still and mirror the ambitions of the world for which it no longer cared.

Well, all that is only half true. I was indeed on a mental holiday, but inwardly I was debating whether I should in fact, apply for a commission. So why was I hesitating? I had, by now, become so aware of different ranks working together in hospitals, and seen the class divide between officers and the rest, that I now knew that what I wanted, was not to be cut off from 'the rest'. That was why I had chosen to join the Army at the bottom. The desert of Libya with its huge message of waste and emptiness was still haunting my soul; and the redeeming night I had spent with the sick and the wounded and the shell-shocked, when we all shared each other's fear, helplessness, hope and despair was still vivid. Both had changed my view of God and humanity for ever.

So now, at the end of my recruits' training, I was marched before an NCO to determine my future in the army. 'You will be posted to the RASC [Royal Army Service Corps], where you can become either a driver or a clerk.' 'What education have you?' 'Harrow School and Balliol College Oxford', I replied. 'Well then, you had better be a clerk.' When my posting came through I was labelled as an 'issuer', but as I never issued anything, I can't be sure what that meant. But then Harrow School, which I had tried to by-pass, took a hand and altered my course, My old Headmaster, Paul Vellacott, had been appointed Director of Political Warfare in Cairo. He invited me to lunch, and urged me to join his set up, with the hope of being sent into enemy occupied Europe to work with a resistance movement. This sounded more interesting than being an issuer, so I agreed.

I spent 10 more days in the Suez Canal, doing fatigues and guards and then came a turning point in my life. The posting to PWE [Political Warfare Executive] arrived. I wrote a letter home, 'I am now finally launched. It is good to feel my brain ticking again, and to be mastering new fields of knowledge. I have put in an application for a commission at the beginning of the week; 80% of candidates fail, but now that I am in this show, I am quite willing to stay, in any capacity. I had dinner with Julian last night and we drank two very good bottles of Alsace wine.'

Julian was engaged to my sister Marjorie, and had emigrated to New Zealand before the war and bought a farm, where they were planning to live and bring up a family. He was now in Cairo with the New Zealand forces and on days off we used to play squash, then go out to dinner together at whatever restaurant we could find which still had a bottle of German wine. Comforted by the wine, we would then moan or laugh about the army, and dream about family life and setting the world to rights after the war. I remember Julian saying, 'the army teaches you two things: smartness and resignation'.

Writing home for Christmas, I was able to share my own good news that the selection board had accepted me for training as an officer, and a message to Marjorie saying that by the time they received my letter, Julian would probably be sitting in the family circle. So it turned out! 'Our family', I wrote, 'will be gathered up into the angels' song at Christmas, – Glory to God in the Highest, and on earth peace, goodwill towards men. I expect each one of us has found that the war has knocked us about; and it seems to me that with each knocking, one is able to be more in love with God's goodwill! That is the opposite of being pious! God knocks down one's piety, and tramples on it, and seems to release the springs of natural behaviour and spontaneous friendship, and the fullness of human life. Since I joined the army, this vision has developed week by week.'

My family – two parents, three sisters and four brothers – continued to be the foundation on which I could stand through all these 'changes and chances'. I needed them now more than ever and wrote to tell them so. The most important test I had to get through on the officers' selection board was the psychological interview. My fear about this had grown immensely because of my dread of stammering, which had been the bane of my life. I felt so frightened that I asked God to help me, and I then remembered that it was 10 years to the day and almost to the hour, that I was confirmed, with my family around me. Now, 10 years later I was to take up another responsibility, for Him and not for myself. I clearly remember the Word Association Test, and in particular the word 'cow', to which I promptly responded – BULL. My fear had evaporated and I never thought about my stammer. I was recommended for a commission – which I felt I must now hold from God as well as the King.

My father had, from time to time, been writing to me about his own deep fears and asking me if I could help him find a safe place, where his mind could be peacefully at rest. That night, after my psychological trial, I had a dream about him walking near our family home in Anglesey, and the risen Christ was walking with him. He seemed to be ten years younger. All his fears had gone, and a great joy radiated from his face. I was able to write him a joyful Christmas letter, and, at last, say to him with confidence, ' you were so happy that I became infected with the happiness, and every time I think of you now, it is as I saw you then. Will you take me with you into His presence?'

For my own Christmas I had a few days leave, so I took the train to Beirut and arrived, uninvited, at the Leavitt's house in time for tea on Christmas Eve. I wrote a separate letter to my mother to give her news of Beirut and the Leavitt family, 'Their house was already overfull, but without a moment's hesitation I was received into the family bosom, and a camp bed was set up in the last remaining corner of the last spare room. Helen looks even more beautiful than her famed namesake. She is 15, very vivacious and quite a handful. Marga has left for America, and men's hearts are breaking all round her. I didn't know that I was in love with her, until I found out that she had gone'.

So that was my Christmas, surrounded by the warmth of home and family, until I returned to life in The Officer Cadet Training Unit. The drill parade became my highlight – instructors descended 'like ravening wolves seeking whom they may devour'. 'You, Sir, you're idle! I'll turn you inside out, Sir. Gentlemen, you're an 'eap. ' I managed to escape their attention for a week, but it was impossible to remain immune for long. The inevitable happened the second week.

'You Sir, you're like a sack of potatoes tied up in the middle'. Then on a cautionary word of command my left foot twitched a little in anticipation. 'You're bone idle, Sir. You're stupid. You've the brains of a rocking horse.' I was put on a charge of 'extreme idleness while on drill parade', and paid for it with half an hour's punishment drill which consisted mainly of marking time.

Then, over Easter, a complete contrast – I went to Jerusalem to stay with Dr and Mrs Altounian. I wrote to my parents, 'Mrs Altounian is the sister of R G Collingwood, who taught me most of what I know about philosophy. Her husband was a close friend of T E Lawrence, and he let me read a book by T.E.L. which cannot be published before 1950, and is about what happened when he joined the RAF. It's the first book I have ever read which captures the life of an 'other rank'. All the obscenity is there, all the foul talk and the bullying and the frightened, beaten personalities, who gradually win through to the comradeship and happiness which is on the other side of the picture. Few men would have the courage to give up the career of 'Lawrence of Arabia' and disappear into another name and a life of fatigues and drill parades. But he did it to lose himself and find himself again; he took the beating and won the prize. You must read it one day. It's called 'The Mint','

I can see [in retrospect] that I was going through something of a similar experience. I think I have to admit that the OCTU had been good for me. When I joined the army there were just two things I didn't want to do. The one, train as a recruit in a squad of Middle East natives; the ʽr, to go through the long grind of training as an infantry ʽr. Having been forced to face the things I was fright- ʽ, I found they were just the things I needed for the training of myself as a person. So I can't help believing in the hand of God over it all; and if over my own small troubles, why not over the troubles of all people and nations. He is an exciting God because his love is ruthless. If he sees that you must pass through some valley to reach the hilltop opposite, then however much you may shrink and cry at the valley's edge, through it you must, and shall go.

So now, having taken a beating I was given a prize. I became commander of my Cadet Company for the last fortnight's training. I would be leading the passing out parade and have a Sam Brown presented to me by the Inspecting Officer! But far more important to me was that the timid cadet who started OCTU 4 months ago was now considered to have the makings of an officer. [My own 'veteran' brothers may be smiling indulgently!] There was still a lot to learn before I acquired the military *savoir faire* of the average private, but I knew now that it could be done.

One week later, I wrote home, and shared with my parents my lifelong agony about my stammer, 'As company commander, I soon got into the idea of delegating everything to everybody else. But last night came my most alarming task: a speech at dinner, proposing the health of the CO and officers It really went off pretty well. They started laughing with the first sentence, and never stopped until the end. They called it 'the laugh a line' speech, the best that had ever been made at OCTU, and even the best they had ever heard! You will forgive me repeating all this, because you know that speech making is for me the hardest ordeal, and therefore the greatest satisfaction when it goes well.'

Then came the last day of OCTU and the passing out parade, with self all polished up to the eyes, and exuding smartness from every crease and button. The Brigadier marches on. S.E.V. goes left right left right. Halt. Salute. 'Company present and ready for inspection Sir.'

Brigadier: 'What is your name?
SEV: 'Verney, Sir'.
Brigadier: 'What regiment are you going into?'
SEV: Intelligence Corps, Sir.'
Brigadier: 'What do you think about Infantry after this course?'
SEV: 'I've learnt to admire them very much, Sir.'
Brigadier: 'You should apply for a transfer, you've missed your vocation.'

Then the inspection and the march past, with self leading and yelling above the noise of the Band 'A Company, by the right, in succession eyes right by platoons', and the platoon commanders taking it up behind, 'No 1 platoon, eyes right.' 'No 2 platoon, eyes right.' Finally myself 'A Company. Halt. Company will advance, left turn. Order Arms. Stand at ease.'

Then came my own great moment. Adjutant. 'Officer Cadet Verney.' SEV goes left right, left right, with arms almost jerking out of their sockets. Halt, and the parade ground shakes as the right foot snaps in! [What nobody knew except me was that one of my puttees began slipping]. Salute: up, two three, down. [Good heavens! Can this really be me?]. We shake hands, and I take off my white belt and scabbard, and the Brigadier straps on to me the most lovely Sam Brown, shining like a mirror in the spring sunshine. Back to my place. The Brigadier talks to us. [He is a VC DSO MC].

The Band strikes up 'Old Lang Syne' and we march past in slow time, and out into the ranks of His Majesty's officers.

WAR WITH THE ARMY –
THE CRETAN RESISTANCE

ઉsingleton

It was decided that I should be sent to Crete because I had started studying Ancient Greek at Oxford, and it was hoped that the Germans would not be able to detect any difference.

At last! Action. The British navy took us across from Tobruk on a moonless night, and landed us on the southern coast of Crete. It was August 17th 1944.

Crete, at that time was part of German occupied Europe. The Cretan Resistance, with a number of British liaison officers, was operating in three mountain areas, and with a network of contacts in the villages and towns. The *antartes,* as we were called in Greek, or the brigands, as we were known to the Germans, avoided any direct contact with the German troops, but carried out acts of sabotage, and then vanished, and came back to control the countryside as soon as the Germans and Italians returned to their barracks. By these tactics, we pinned down a large number of enemy troops who could otherwise have been sent to fight elsewhere; by October 1943 there were 273,000 Germans, 54,000 Bulgarians and 18,000 Italians stationed in Greece. I think there were about 12 of us who had been recruited by the British army, but we had the brave Cretan people on our side, without whom the story would have been very different.

Our policy of harassment led to fierce reactions from the German high command. In March 1942 they published the orders called 'Atonement Operations'. One German death would be expiated by 100 Greek deaths. Captured rebels were to be hanged or shot. All troops must be trained to apply unconditional harshness. No false sentimentality! 'Villages suspected of giving assistance to the rebels shall be destroyed. If it is not possible to capture those participating in the rebellion, general reprisals may be made, for instance, shooting the male inhabitants of the surrounding villages'. On October 18th 1942, Hitler published a new order. 'All enemy commandos shall be massacred to the last man. Even if they surrender, no pardon shall be granted. It is strictly forbidden to keep any of these people in military care or in prisoner of war camps, even as a temporary measure'. At that time General Lohr was in command of the German forces in Greece; he was described by his adjutant as 'the most noble and refined man I have ever met; if he did have a flaw, it was in his acceptance of what was ordered from above'. On October 28th, he issued his addendum to the Führer's order. 'There are no half measures. Notions of 'the heroism of a freedom loving nation' etc are misplaced. Most precious German blood is at stake here. I expect every officer to be personally involved in ensuring that this order is carried out with brutal harshness.'

Crete had experienced that harshness earlier, in the massacre of the entire Jewish population who were crammed into a boat which was then taken out to sea and sunk; and later in the shooting of male inhabitants in villages.

My brief was to create a mutiny in the German army, and to break down the morale of the German troops. [In 1918 the First World War was brought to an end by a mutiny – I needed to remember that.] I was to be disguised as a Cretan and assume the persona of a cattle dealer. I would be 'armed' with printed propaganda and a pistol which had to be kept cocked. I was expected to identify Germans who might be likely to defect; so it was necessary that I should somehow live among them in Khania, the capital of Western Crete, only returning to the mountains when it was necessary. With me there would be a German-English interpreter, George Colin, an NCO from the South African army. What nobody knew, except him and me, was that he was a Jewish refugee from Hitler's Germany, and that he was therefore running a horrific extra risk.

As our ship approached the coast of Crete, the engine throbbed through the darkness, and I imagined that all the Germans for miles around would be gathering on the shore to greet us. Then from a little cove under the huge mountains, we saw a flashing light with the agreed signal for all clear. Our welcome party was an excited and noisy group of *antartes,* led by our commanding officer, Tom Dunbabbin, who was a fellow of All Souls College, Oxford. Tom got us to hurry along, and ordered 'no smoking', as a minimum and tardy precaution against being spotted by the Germans! After 20 minutes our stores were unloaded, and those going back to Egypt had embarked. The navy pulled out to sea, and the rest of us shouldered our rucksacks and other gear and started on a long, steep climb.

My first impression of Crete was the scent of the thyme that filled the night air, and it remains, for me, the most evocative of scents. By dawn we had reached a safe resting place, and after a short rest, Tom introduced me to Markos Drakakis who was to be my Cretan guide. He was a shepherd boy from Asi Gonia, a nearby village. We were about the same age, and from that moment on, he came with me everywhere, by day and by night, and risked his life for me many times over. Through him I came to know the courage and generosity of the Cretan people, who, almost without exception, were ready to give everything, including themselves, for the freedom of their country.

The next day Markos led me and George, my German interpreter, down from the mountains and into Khania. As we walked into the town we passed some German soldiers, and my knees wobbled with fright. This was the first time that our disguise was being tested and I felt as though it was transparently obvious that I was an English officer. But nobody gave us a second glance. We walked through the centre of the town, and down to the harbour; then up a little alley way, and a flight of steps to knock on the door of a Venetian house, with a balcony overlooking the harbour. The door was opened by Mitsos Antonakakis, and behind him was his hospitable wife, Artemisia. They welcomed us as honoured guests, and as liberators. Their house became our headquarters, or, more truly, their home became our home. They treated us like sons, with no shadow of fear for themselves and the appalling danger they were running. They showed us an escape route over the roof, in case the Germans came to the house, but there could have been no escape for them. They were real heroes – light hearted because they had let themselves go and were following the tradition of their ancestors in driving out the hated invader to restore their freedom.

The following day we met other Cretans of the same calibre, including Tassos Ninolakis who offered to carry our propaganda into town, hidden under a load of carob beans in the back of a lorry. Then there were two handsome brothers who came down from the mountains; one of them – Antonis could run so fast that he was able to catch a hare running uphill. Chief among my contacts was Kostas Mitsotakis who later became Prime Minister of Greece. He was at this time a young lawyer who spoke fluent German, and he made the arrangements for George and myself to meet with Germans whom he believed to be anti-Hitler. So we formed a cell and this small group became my gang.

The first German I met was a middle aged man who had been a member of the German parliament before Hitler's rise to power; He hated meeting us and appearing to betray his country, but this antipathy was overwhelmed by his loathing of the Nazis and his eagerness to work for the creation of a new Germany. I was moved by his courage and honesty. We met in the Antonakakis house, but quickly realised that this was dangerous.

The next man was a young Austrian officer, in the Counter Espionage Service, and I met him in his office! He too hated the Nazis and was outraged that they had overrun his country and forced Austrians to serve in their armies.

The third man was a German Sergeant Major who had fallen in love with a Cretan girl; she had opened his eyes to see Hitler and the Nazis, as Cretans saw them.

These three represented three categories which we could focus on; first, democratic Germans; secondly, other nationals forced to serve with the German army; and thirdly, men who had fallen in love with Cretan girls.

After a week in Khania, I went back to a village 'safe house' to get some 'stuff', and there I found a letter from home. The second front was raging in France, and I learnt that my brother Hugh had been seriously wounded in the head, and had 'got it bad'. Black revenge swept through me and I wanted to go out and kill a German; but reason prevailed, and as this could certainly lead to a massacre of Cretans, I returned quietly to my work.

Our activities and propaganda had gained momentum,

and begun to worry the German counter espionage service – where of course we had a well placed friend. They began to search for us, and I had three narrow escapes.

The first was when Markos and I were travelling into Khania on a bus. The bus was stopped at a control post, and German soldiers made us queue up outside the bus to be searched. I described what happened in a letter written soon after war ended. 'I was carrying in my pockets a pistol, a spare magazine of ammunition, a bag of gold sovereigns and a little English bible. I arranged with Markos that he should go through first, and then slip back to take my things off me. But the guard stopped him coming back. I was then fourth in the queue from the Germans and about three yards away. The driver's door of the bus was open, so I took my pistol out of my pocket, and dropped it under his seat amongst the tools. It fell with an awful clang, and the driver immediately guessed who I was, and called a pretty girl passenger to sit on the seat over the pistol. When it was my turn to be searched, I showed my forged identity card, and raised my hands above my head. The guard patted down my sides and over my pockets, but luckily did not recognise the feel of my spare ammunition magazine. My disguise was 100% perfect'. But my recklessness was 100% stupid! When we got to the bus station in Khania, Markos went to reclaim my pistol. The brave and resourceful bus driver murmured, 'Tell him to be more careful next time'!

The second escape was an even closer shave. George and I had been taken to spend the night in a factory, with the promise that someone would bring us breakfast. Morning came – but no breakfast. Then we heard noises of banging on doors and dogs barking. We learned later that the Germans were doing a house to house search for us. All the men in the streets of Khania were rounded up and crowded into a sports field, where they were searched and then marked on the forehead before they were allowed to go home. Meanwhile, soldiers with dogs were carrying on with their house to house search. George and I heard them coming up our street. We climbed up through a trap door into the attic of the factory, and pulled up the ladder behind us. Then followed two hours when I was more terrified than I have ever been, before or since. We heard them coming closer and closer. If they had found us, I could not have stood up. My legs were like jelly. My watch stopped – it was a self winding watch which had never stopped before and has never stopped since. Then they arrived at our factory, and banged on the iron shutter. And then ... passed on up the street. Apparently someone had called out to them that it was an empty warehouse. It was, by now, coming up to midday, and I guess the soldiers were hot, tired and hungry.

The third incident involved something very rare in wartime Crete and also shows the darker side of the Cretan character. Markos and I arrived one evening at a village, and called at a 'safe house' to ask for something to eat. After supper they pressed us to stay the night, but as there was bright moonlight, we decided to walk on. Half an hour after we had left, the house was surrounded by German troops who burnt down the house because they were convinced that we were hiding in the chimney. It was immediately presumed that a traitor had informed the Germans. Traitors were rare in Crete. In general, one trusted the whole population. Any traitor was hated and despised. After the war, the suspects were put on trial, and when a judge did not condemn them to death, for lack of evidence, the public rushed into the court-room and cut off their heads.

That night Markos and I were walking over the mountains to the Monastery of Arkardi, high up in the centre of Crete, because all the officers of the Resistance were meeting there. The monks were heart and soul in our support against the Germans, as their forefathers had been against the Turks, a century earlier, and provided havens for us all over Crete. This particular meeting was arranged because the news was coming through that the Germans were planning to withdraw from Greece. As it transpired, they had intended this to include a total withdrawal from Crete, but time had been against them, and half their garrison was left behind. Eastern Crete became free, and their army of occupation was concentrated around Khania where George and I were working.

But while Markos and I were up in the mountains, I learned that some of our gang had been captured by the Germans – including George, Tassos and Kostas Mitsotakis. My blood ran cold. The Germans had set up a decoy, who pretended that he wanted to talk to us, and while I was away the others agreed to meet and brought him to the house where they were all gathered. Hard behind the decoy came soldiers, who arrested them and incarcerated them in Aghia Prison.

I recognised the extreme danger they were in, but also knew that to rescue them by force was impossible. So I wrote immediately to the German Commander, signing myself 'Major Stephens' even though I was only a 2nd Lieutenant. I made it clear that if a hair on their heads was harmed, there would be dire consequences – the German prisoners of war in Cairo would be castrated. My threats were reiterated by genuine high ranking British officers, and proved successful. Negotiations began for an exchange of prisoners, and five months later my gang members were released, unharmed.

Our work in Khania was now gravely hampered by the concentration of German soldiers, and for the rest of the war Markos and I lived in different villages, outside the town with our own group of *antartes*. We carried on with our propaganda, and began publishing a German language newspaper called 'Kreta Post'. It was edited in a remote cave above Khania by a journalist named Xenophon Hadjigrigoris. At the same time we were hearing about a battalion of Italians who hated their German allies, and so Markos and I hatched up a plan. We went to the Italian hospital to meet the colonel who was in charge of this battalion; I pretended to be a patient and lay on the operating table while the doctor examined me, and the Colonel stood beside us. We spoke in French, and agreed that at midnight, on a prearranged date, the Colonel would lead three of his companies into the mountains, while the fourth would go to a little harbour on the seashore, and be taken off in a caique. Captain John Stanley, one of my Resistance colleagues, would bring the caique round the coast to Kastelli Kissamou, while I led the other party along mountain paths to meet them there. The operation happened as we had planned, and then we marched our 'prisoners of war' across the island to the south coast, where they were to be taken off by the British navy.

The only hitch was that the Cretan villagers refused to let them pass through carrying their arms, so that we had to turn back to Kastelli at the first attempt, to deposit their arms in two empty warehouses. Markos and I had to stay to guard the arms, and it was here that I experienced, for the only time in Crete, the political schism which eventually caused such a bitter civil war in the rest of Greece. The Communist sympathisers heard about the arms which had been deposited, and collected outside the warehouses to demand their share of them. Markos and I stood firm in front of the locked doors and refused to yield, making it clear that they belonged to Allied Headquarters in Cairo. It was a dangerous and distressing moment, to face as potential enemies, Cretans with whom we had felt ourselves so deeply united.

During those last months of the war, I was becoming more aware of other 'opposites' in my Cretan friends. Their outstanding national characteristic was *philotimo,* which means a love of honour, or a deep respect. This made them the bravest of fighters, the most loyal of allies and the best of friends. But it had its darker side. For example, one day one of my *antartes* asked if he could have a weekend's leave to go home to kill his cousin. His cousin had stolen his sheep. For centuries, in Crete, sheep had been the symbol of a man's status, and if they were stolen, then his sense of honour demanded that he kill the thief. This would then set up a blood feud between the family of the thief and the family of the killer. In this instance, I was able to diffuse the situation by explaining to my man that I was refusing permission for home leave, and so his honour was satisfied.

Another example of 'honour' involved a parish priest who came to see me with a deputation. In their village there was an Italian soldier who had deserted, and he did odd jobs for the villagers. The Italian had been paying too much attention to the priest's wife, and had indeed been found hiding under her bed. And so there was a dilemma; if the priest killed him, as honour demanded, he would no longer be allowed by the law of the church, to celebrate Holy Communion; but if he did not kill the Italian, parishioners would not come to Holy Communion. He had a stout stick in his hand, and after we had debated the matter, it was made clear to all that the Italian soldier was a prisoner of war, and we could not allow him to be killed, but the priest could flog him publicly, and so the demands of honour would be met.

Such a very earthy encounter with the Greek Church was soon overwhelmed by another, in which the central mystery of the orthodox faith was enacted. The war in Crete was coming to an end on the Tuesday after Easter. On the Eve of Easter, we were all bursting and choking with excitement as we came to the midnight service in Kastelli Kissamou. The whole population was packed into the church and overflowing, while the priest led us in prayer and thanksgiving. Then, he led us out under the open sky, and on the stroke of midnight, April 1st 1945, he cried out 'CHRIST IS RISEN', and we all shouted in reply 'TRULY, HE IS RISEN'. And then followed such a response as never before can have greeted the Risen Lord. MACHINE GUNS, PISTOLS, and ROCKETS were fired into the air. LANDMINES were exploded. Everyone had arms hidden for the war, with which they now welcomed THE PRINCE OF PEACE. We sang 'Christ is risen from among the Dead Corpses. By Death he has trampled on Death. And to those in the Tombs, he has granted the Free Gift of Life.'

On the Monday morning, those of us who had served in the Resistance, went into Khania, and met up with our friends. Inevitably, we began to arrange a party for this last night of the war. And the idea emerged that we should invite those members of the German Intelligence Service who had been trying to catch us over all these months and years. So we did. And they came. There were many introductions. 'Yes, I am Major Stephens!' They were astonished that there were so few of us; they had imagined hundreds; they thought they would be meeting dignified mature officers, not a gang of lads in their twenties, with not a trace of dignitas in sight. There was dancing and wine, and as the night wore on they left us, and went home – to become our prisoners the following morning.

*

But this festivity was not the end of the story. I was asked to stay on in Khania to open an Information Centre. I hired a cafe, and after a day or two, a packet of photographs arrived. They turned out to be the very first pictures from the concentration camps which had just been liberated. There were horrendous scenes of starving bodies, and as I pinned them up on the walls, I could hardly believe them myself. Our German prisoners of war were still free to move about the streets of Khania because we had no manpower to keep them shut up. They looked at the pictures with total incredulity. They had grown used to the evil propaganda of Goebbels over the last ten years, and concluded that these photographs were nothing more than British propaganda. Some angry soldiers hid a grenade under my car – which fortunately did not go off. They were presumably acting out of loyalty to their country and respect for the Third Reich. But by the end of April, the Third Reich had disintegrated, Hitler committed suicide, in his bunker, on April 30th 1945. A day later, on May 1st, exactly a month after Easter Day, Goebbels and his wife committed suicide in the same bunker, after first murdering their six children.

REFLECTION OF MY TIME IN CRETE

૬✦ई

Fifty years later I was back in Khania for a party. My Greek gang wanted to celebrate, the anniversary of their capture and release from Aghia Prison! We gathered on the beach, ate fish and drank wine until the early hours of the morning. The two handsome brothers came down from the mountains, looking as fit as ever with two impressive handle bar moustaches. I called in to see Artemisia, whose house was close by. She was now blind and confused; she felt me all over, and kept on saying [in Greek], 'But Stephanos, you are not wearing your battledress'. Her maid and grandchildren looked after me, and recounted everything they had heard with much embroidery – even showing me hiding places which I had never seen before!

But there was one thing left for me to do. Markos Drakakis had moved to Athens, where he had been working as a policeman since the end of the war. He had been unable to come to the party because he was dying of cancer, so I took the morning plane and went over to see him. His wife and family greeted me with open arms, smiling faces and eyes full of tears. On their mantelpiece there were two photographs with an icon in between them. One was of me, aged 26, in uniform at the end of the war. The other was of Markos, aged 28, in uniform at the end of the war. Between them was an icon of Christ. These three had been standing together for 50 years, at the heart of their family home.

As I looked at them, I suddenly saw that being a soldier and following the way of Christ was not a problem for

Markos. In his mind, he and I were risking our lives for the freedom of the Cretan people and Christ was with us. Markos, while I was agonising, knew instinctively, that our fight for freedom had been 'in his name'. He and I had been able to empower one another, and make each other capable of heroism, by letting go the 'I' and becoming the 'I am'. So, finally, through the eyes of my brother in war it came to me in an 'unblinding flash' that Jesus was at home, both among pacifists working to heal wounds, and among soldiers fighting to liberate prisoners. Behind the coincidence of opposites, Love was alive and holding them both together.

PART 3

FALLING IN LOVE

❦

The war ended on May 8th 1945. The sun was shining and the whole Cretan countryside was ablaze with spring flowers. By the autumn all the British officers who had been in Crete during the war were married to beautiful Cretan girls – all except myself.

It was not that I hadn't fallen in love with them. In a sense I fell in love with them all, I learned to dance, and every evening there was a party; and as I danced and held those beautiful and mysterious creatures in my arms, our bodies moved together in an ecstasy of desire. They were as fascinated by us as we were by them. We were, for them, the heroes who had risked their lives and brought freedom to their country, and who now beckoned to them to leave their island and come with us to enjoy the affluence and prestige of 'Great Britain'! They were, for us, the female partners of whom we had dreamed, during those months of stress and warfare, and who now beckoned us to days and nights of love and peace. Those British friends of mine who let themselves go into Cretan marriages were braver and more natural than I was, and, for the most part, formed stable relationships and gave birth to creative and attractive Anglo-Greek children, For my part, I was ready for romance but not yet for marriage.

I had returned to Oxford, in September 1946, to continue my course in philosophy and history – interrupted 7 years earlier by the outbreak of war. My ancient university continued on its way as though the war had been a hiccup, and I remember the opening words of my first lecture on Ancient Greek history, given incidentally by a professor who had himself taken part in the Greek Resistance, 'After the battle of Aegospotami', he began, 'the question facing the Athenians. . .' I gasped. Aegospotami! Where and when was that? Who was fighting whom, and about what?

But I quickly discovered that this seven year break had opened my mind; the questions raised by the philosophers and historians were no longer academic questions which a schoolboy had to answer to pass an exam. They were real and vital questions with which I, as a man, had wrestled through seven years of the war. Nothing could be more exciting now than to study how Plato had asked and answered them in his generation, in that country which I had come to know and love. 'Nothing'? But one thing *was* more exciting, and it actually began to happen.

My youngest sister was working in Oxford as an Occupational Therapist and one of her colleagues was called Scilla Schwerdt. We nicknamed them 'the Therapim'. I found myself immediately attracted to Scilla, but at a level deeper than my romances. I eventually realised that the attraction was mutual and mysterious. Scilla had been struck down by polio as a teenager, and had been paralysed for two years, but after a successful operation she returned to active life. She walked with a slight limp and seemed to be enriched by the experience of her own helplessness. Because she was offering me her vulnerability, I could stop pretending and I could recognise my own vulnerability. Vulnerability is literally the ability to be wounded, the ability to feel the pain of our wounds, and so the capacity to understand other people's wounds and to share their pain, which is the meaning of the word 'compassion' – 'to suffer with'. It is compassion which makes possible the depth of Love between human beings, and which now enabled the to and fro of Love to begin between us.

I say 'to begin', because this was 1946, and men still saw themselves as the superior sex. The British Empire still ruled in India. We had just won the war. It was hardly conceivable that men should do housework, or look after the children. But this was the year when hundreds of thousands of us were getting married, including six of my own siblings. A sexual revolution was in full flood, pointing us towards a new equality of men and women, a new discovery of the reality of love, and so towards a deeper perception of the being of God.

I found myself doubly involved in this journey of discovery, for at the same time as I became a husband I was accepted by the Church of England for training to become a priest. My wife and I moved to Cambridge where she gave birth to our son, and where for two years I studied theology.

Again I began to be aware of something mysterious and amazing, that in both these aspects of my life – the family and the church – it was the same truth which was coming to meet me; the reality of a Love which was very different from what I had expected. My conventional pictures of the macho husband and of the 'good Jesus' had to be *broken,*and to give place to an understanding of Love which arose *out of that very brokenness.* Such an understanding has to come slowly and painfully, from the experience of our own emptiness. 'Narrow is the gate' said Jesus, 'and the way which leads to Life is beset with affliction, and few there be who find it', For it leads through death; it could be the death of ones self image, or the physical death of somebody deeply loved, or through our own physical death.

Snakes and Ladders

Falling in love! The whole body comes alive, and the whole personality. It is the setting free of myself – my psyche – through contact with one another. As Sappho, one of the early poets of Europe, wrote around 600 BC, 'Love is irresistible and bittersweet, and it makes me tremble'. Like the Quakers in the presence of God! But why bittersweet? Because falling in love is followed by 'being in love', the people who have fallen in love now live together; they have to live *in love* as one might say that fish live in water and birds live in the air. Hitherto they have lived in egocentricity. Now they are required to leave their egocentricity behind, to 'put their psyche for their friends'! To listen and understand the other's story; to laugh with them; to cry with them and feel their pain; to trust them; to care for them; to help set free their true selves. In this living together they discover, most bitter of all, that the egocentric self is so far from perfect as to be in itself incapable of this love,

St John, 'the disciple whom Jesus loved' as he remembered that love, summed up his experience by saying that Jesus was a ladder between time and eternity and he chose to share our vulnerability. He did this for all those who would follow him on the way through the narrow gate, *His vulnerability would set free our vulnerability, and so the possibility that it could be transformed into compassion.*

CLIFTON, NOTTINGHAM
By our own hands and God's grace

ౢ≈ఇ

After I was ordained and had served for two years learning the traditional job of a clergyman, the Bishop, Russell Barry, gave me my first posting, and sent me to a new housing estate at Clifton, which was being built as part of the programme to re-house the population of Britain after the devastation of the war.

The concrete houses were being mass produced, a whole street at a time. When I arrived there were already some hundreds of people living there but as yet no shops, no pubs; the first school was just opening. In appointing me as curate-in-charge to the new area the Bishop said 'The important thing is to get a priest there, and the church gathering round him. You will probably have to do without a church building for 20 years'.

This difference between the *church* and the *church building* was something which my wise old Bishop saw as the key to what I had to do, but which I, as an inexperienced young curate only knew in theory. Like everybody else, I understood the word 'church' to mean a building, and being a Christian to mean going to a church building. One would judge how many Christians there were in a parish by how many people 'went to church'. Yet I knew from my theological studies that the church meant the people. The original word in Greek was '*ecclesia*' [*ek* = out, *kletos*=called] that is how the new Christians saw themselves – they were 'called

91

out' to set people free. That is the truth which was now to be shown to us once again in Clifton.

My wife and I with our son Robin moved into one of the concrete council houses. She was pregnant again, and during the 6 years we spent in Clifton she gave birth to our three daughters. The world of nappies, prams and toddlers was something we shared with almost every other household, for we were all young couples setting up our new homes. It was a time of hope; but for many of the mothers it was also a time of great loneliness, for the housing estate was not a community. I remember visiting one young mum who told me that she was deeply depressed, and wanted to throw herself into the River Trent. I took her across the road and introduced her to another young mum who said 'But, I too, feel I want to throw myself into the Trent'.

On that first week-end, as we moved into this neighbour-hood which was, not yet, a community of neighbours, I was confronted by a question mark. What does the curate-in-charge do on a Sunday if he has no church? So I wrote out a notice, and stuck it up with a drawing pin on an old oak tree which was being used as a notice board, to say that there would be a celebration of the Holy Communion in our house on the Sunday morning, and that anyone would be welcome. In response to that invitation 6 people came. We broke bread. 'Take and eat this, in remembrance of me'. We drank wine. 'This is my blood shed for you'. We knew 'where two or three are gathered together in my name, there am I'.

So the church on Clifton estate was born. As we remembered Jesus Christ, he came that morning out of eternity and into that council house, and gave himself to us.

Those 6 people were not chosen by me, but they had, between them, the gifts needed to start being the church, so that a year later, the *Daily Mail* could write 'a miracle has happened here'. They had started Youth Clubs and a Sunday school where 300 children were being taught the story of Jesus. Men and women had discovered a new purpose and happiness in life. And a church building was being built by voluntary labour.

How did that come about? Before starting work, I had travelled around England picking up ideas from other housing estates. When I went to Leeds, one day, I happened to get onto the wrong bus, and was set down a mile from my destination. Another man travelling in the bus, offered to show me the way, and as we walked, he told me that he and a group of friends were building their own houses together, by voluntary labour and the pooling of their skills. We arrived at the building site, and when I saw what was happening, I knew that a coincidence had shown me how the church was to be built at Clifton. 'And never forget', said the Lord God, 'that it was your mistake, and my idea'.

This revelation that God intervenes in human affairs through our mistakes was not new. It was written down many centuries ago by Julian of Norwich, a woman hermit.

'Our Lord God showed me that a deed shall be done, and Himself shall do it, and I shall do nothing but sin, and my sin shall not hinder His goodness working'.

The insight that God works through coincidence was also by no means new. William Temple, the great Archbishop of Canterbury, whom we have already remembered, had said '*I have learnt that when I pray coincidences happen*'.

Now this revelation and this insight was coming alive in my own experience, and as I 'remember', I glimpse the backside of God's glory, as did Moses, in the Book of Exodus. His presence, which we came to know in our relations with each other, is *not just a psychological state between us*. Love takes the initiative, and brings together the two sides of a coincidence, and works through our mistakes and our emptiness.

The Bishop had said to me 'gather people around you who will BE the church. That is the priority. You may have to wait for 20 years to BUILD a church'. But now it was beginning to appear that for this new neighbourhood, which was not yet a community, to *build a church might offer a way to be the church*. It would bring us together and use our gifts and skills, and so, weld us into a community as we worked together.

So, a Christmas letter went to every family in the new housing estate.

'Are you a bricklayer, a plasterer, a joiner, a cabinet maker, a plumber, a decorator, an electrician or a glazier? Do you know anything about roofing, concrete mixing, scaffolding, heating installation, carving, painting sewing, embroidery, metal work, carpet-making? Or are you like me, quite unskilled in anything, but could get cracking with a pick and shovel, and help dig foundations?

If you are, will you come and help build a church?

Nobody is going to build it for us. Suppose we decided to build it ourselves? A modest church and hall would cost about £30,000. We haven't got the money – but we are all young and active. We could give £1 worth of labour on long summer evenings, and together offer £10,000 worth of work. Then we could say to others, 'Help us to help ourselves. Give us £20,000 to buy materials'.

We would argue out the scheme together, pool our ideas,

ask for criticism and advice. About 60 people turned out on a cold winter night. We got enough offers of help to make sure the scheme could go ahead, and formed a council of skilled tradesmen to organise the building operation for us.

What did that say about the word 'church'? Nobody was badgering them to 'come to church'; we were asking them for help – help to BE the church and to build the church. We weren't asking them to come and worship an old man in the sky. We were asking them to build a centre amongst their new homes where they could bring their babies to be blessed by the Truth that we belong together; where they could come on their wedding day and offer themselves 'for richer for poorer, to love and to cherish till death us do part'; where they could bring their loved ones who had died and trust them into the arms of eternal mercy. Most people want such a centre, and always have done, since history began. But not everyone feels themselves called to follow Jesus through the narrow gate and along the difficult way of compassion. Or perhaps they really are called, and respond using their own metaphors for the Father's 'ecclesia'.

At the time, I did not understand any of these things, and the next 6 years at Clifton were a time of agony and ecstasy. Agony, as I experienced for the first time what the Church really was, those few who were 'called' and sent on 'special service', not unlike my being sent to Crete to create a mutiny among enemy forces! But here at Clifton we did not have a leader who stood outside us and gave commands, but one who lived inside us, and is the spirit of what he has commanded, 'Love one another as I have loved you'. To rediscover this was the ecstasy.

The agony was that most of our fellow citizens simply ignored us, and that so many who started out with us, lost heart and gave up. This had been the agony of our Founder around 2000 years ago, and continues to be the disillusion of his ecclesia. *But who wants to be illusioned?* Would we not rather that our eyes were opened to the truth? 'My spirit', said Jesus, 'is the spirit of Truth, of Reality'. So also is the Hindu spirit, for their great prayer is 'from unreality lead us to Reality'. And so, as I began to learn at Clifton, is the spirit of Everyman and of Everywoman, who wouldn't 'come to church', but who wanted a church to be there. They did not want to say prayers, in a language which was unintelligible and seemed to commit them to a lot of nonsense. Their prayer had to be in their own language. A bricklayer could pray through laying bricks, an artist could pray through painting a picture, and a carpenter could pray through sawing wood. There are two valuable circles of response around a church building; those who 'come to church' and take part week by week in the worship, and those who come very occasionally or never, but who are grateful for the symbol, and the Truth for which it stands.

In our new Church we hung, as the central symbol, an empty cross, roughly in the proportions of a human figure with outstretched arms. The man who made it fitted a strip of light along the back of the cross so that it shone out and reminded us of the presence of the Risen Christ. Some months after the building was finished, the widow of a man who had just died came to ask me to arrange his funeral. She had never been inside the church but 'One evening', she told me, 'as I was walking home, I saw the light of the cross shining out through the window of the church'. In her grief, she felt deeply comforted.

But, before that could happen, there had been 5 years of hard work and disillusion. The first summer went with a swing. We dug and built the foundations of the church, and, on June 26th came the laying of the foundation stone. There was a long debate as to who should lay it. All sorts of names were canvassed, including Royalty, Presidents of Republics, Dukes, broadcasters and other celebrities. But we came at last to the best answer. The foundation stone carries the inscription:

> *This stone was laid on 26th July 1953*
> *by*
> *the blacksmith of Clifton village*
> *clerk to the parish church*
> *where God has been worshipped*
> *for a thousand years*
> *and by*
> *a bricklayer of Clifton estate*
> *one of many volunteers who are*
> *by their own hands and God's grace*
> *building a church among their new homes.*
> *'Jesus Christ the same yesterday and today and for ever'.*

The words 'by their own hands and God's grace' were thought of by the mason who carved the stone. 'That's good', he said. 'It just gets it. You must have those words'. Their truth became clearer to us as time went by.

The story of the next four years is not easy to tell. What happened, outwardly, was that most of the volunteers fell away, and there was left a little nucleus of about a dozen builders. The brunt of the work, the long, slow grind, 'the heat and burden of the day', was borne by a few.

And what happened inwardly? They were becoming a ladder between heaven and earth. I didn't know this. They didn't know this. Most of them would have repudiated any such idea! But as they worked through the long summer evenings and the cold winter week-ends, as they met every sort of frustration, and overcame every sort of difficulty, as the years passed and they grew tired, they were offering the work of their own hands to each other, and *God's grace was holding them together.*

The Devil saw it and trembled, for this is the thing he most hates. His style is to attack, darken, and disrupt. He found the chinks in everybody's armour, and twisted each man's best into his worst. Those who had sacrificed most, arrived at the day of consecration most deeply wounded and conscious of failure. But God's grace had been interacting with their work, and on that Day of Consecration, May 19th 1957, he let go our failures and accepted the work. As the service moved towards its completion, there happened to us, what had happened long ago, at the consecration of the temple in Jerusalem:

'It came even to pass, as the trumpeters and singers were as one, to make one sound to be heard in praising and thanking the Lord; for he is good; for his mercy endureth for ever; that then the house was filled with a cloud, even the house of the Lord; so that the priests could not stand to minister by reason of the cloud; for the glory of the Lord had filled the house of God'. [2 Chronicles 5. 13]

'Remembering', after 50 years, I see that the character of God is mediated to us through the kind of church we are. If we are a church run by the clergy, then we are likely to imagine God as a great high priest, or as some other variation of that old authority figure above the sky. If the church is a fellowship where decisions are taken together, a unity, where each person can contribute her or his 'I AM' to the diversity of the whole, then it becomes more likely that we can imagine God as Love, 'in whom,' as St Paul said to the Athenians, 'we live and move and have our being'. The organisation of the church will affect our idea of God, but, conversely, our idea of God will affect the organisation and the character of the church. If we imagine God as an individual person, as some kind of august ruler, then we are more likely to be fundamentalists bound by the letter of his rules, and to be exclusively convinced that our tribe is right and other tribes, who disagree with us, are wrong. *If we imagine God as more personal than any person – as the Love in which individuals become persons* – then, we are more likely to grow together in compassion and forgiveness, and to recognise God in others who are different from ourselves.

So the theory of *God* has a profound effect on the character of the church we build, and the church we are; and for us, at Clifton, that was summed up by the stone-mason who understood that our church was built by our own hands and by God's grace.

Its furnishing reflected that grace. They were free gifts from many people. The Headmistress of one of our schools gave the timber for the altar, which was designed by the man who led the volunteer builders for five years, though he never 'came to church'; it was made at the Portland Training College for the disabled. The font was designed by our architect, who, over 5 years, had encouraged us to go on doing the impossible; he used a beautiful brass bowl and jug, to hold the water for baptism, the gift of a family who had used it as a washing bowl.

Around the altar lies a tapestry kneeler representing the whole creation. It was designed by a teacher of biology, and made by her, with help from others in the parish. On the

99

altar are two silver candlesticks, the work of one of England's leading goldsmiths, and a silver chalice and paten, the work of one of Germany's leading goldsmiths. The works of the English and German craftsmen, placed together on the altar, ten years after the end of the war, cry 'Glory be to God on high, and on earth, Peace'.

One could go on and on listing the furnishings, and remembering how they are the original work of the hands and minds of their makers. At the same time, they reflect the *grace* of God which had built the church with us, not only because they are free gifts, but also because they point towards the Way through suffering to joy, and through death to life.

We had chosen, as our patron saint, St Francis, and the statue of him that greets you, as you enter, was the gift of a doctor in Exeter. When he brought it, neither he nor we knew who it was. Some medieval friar? But, the following morning, as we looked at it again, there, in his hands were the marks of the nails – the stigmata – which Francis received in his body towards the end of his life. Why had we not seen them the evening before? They are the sign of God's compassion. Our patron saint reminded us that our hands, which create and bless, must bear those marks of the nails, even if not visible to our physical eyes.

Supremely, on the ceiling of the church is the great mural painting of 'The Company of Heaven'. It was painted by Pamela Lloyd, a student at the Royal College of Art, who was baptised while working on it. The subject of it was the passage from the Communion service;

Therefore with Angels and Archangels, and with all the company of heaven, we laud and magnify thy glorious name, evermore praising thee and saying, Holy, holy, holy Lord God of Hosts, heaven and earth are full of thy glory. Glory be to thee, O Lord most High. Amen.

For many artists, their work is their means of praying, and Pamela wrote, 'It is my Prayer'. In the greatest works of art, or the very greatest lives, for example, in the life of St Francis of Assisi, in the paintings of Rembrandt, in the music of Bach, we see two things, the prayer made by man and transfiguring that prayer, God's answer. The rest of us make our own clumsy prayers, the deficiencies of which we know well in our own hearts. In Pamela's painting, the first consideration was to lead the eye from the main entrance of the church towards the focus of the church, the great cross above the altar. The final consideration was the subject itself, a great throng of earthly and heavenly worshippers moving, in a joyous mass, singing, playing musical instruments, carrying flowers or simply worshipping in silence. A great cry of homage and happiness. Soft and rich colours were used, and a multitude of figures, because the painting was intended to be an affirmation of faith in the warmth and overflowing generosity of God.

Pamela painted into The Company of Heaven, two little boys who had recently died while she was working on the mural – Brian Howley and Ian Birch, each the only child of their parents. They are shown in their guardian angel's arms.

In Christian art, Judas Iscariot is usually painted in Hell – burning, or in Dante's *Inferno* – freezing. In our Church, in Clifton, he is up there in Heaven. God's mercy has 'rescued him from evil'.

CONSECRATION OF
COVENTRY CATHEDRAL

৾৶৾

In the summer of 1958, Cuthbert Bardsley, the Bishop of Coventry, invited me to become a member of his staff, and to help prepare for the consecration of the new Coventry Cathedral in 1962.

The old medieval cathedral had been destroyed in an air-raid on November 14th 1940. 'All night long the city burned, and her cathedral burned with her' wrote the Provost Dick Howard the next morning.

He wrote later in his book *Ruined and Rebuilt,* 'As I watched the cathedral burning, it seemed to me that I was watching the crucifixion of Jesus, I went with this thought in my mind into the ruins on the morning after the destruction, and there flashed into my mind the deep certainty that the cathedral would rise again with Him through Hitler. God can make good to triumph over evil'. Back at home he found the Bishop waiting, and the first visitor to come, to sympathise in their joint loss was the Minister of the Baptist Church. So it was, in the same night, Hitler destroyed the Cathedral and blew a hole in the side of the Church of England, while Christians rediscovered their unity through the crucifixion of Jesus – a knowledge which found expression later in the building of a chapel of Unity.

'In January 1941', wrote Dick Howard, 'I got Jack Forbes the stonemason to build an altar of stones from the rubble on the site of the high altar, and to set behind it a cross made of charred beams'. Later he had the words *'Father forgive'* carved in huge letters on the wall behind the altar and the charred cross.

He had launched the new cathedral on the way of Forgiveness and Reconciliation. He had, at the same time, shown the meaning of the word Consecration – *in which the opposites of human nature and God's Spirit are made one.* His vision of reconciliation sprang out of his own humility and stubbornness, transformed and made one and consecrated by the Spirit of Jesus.

He was a humble man, and some truth shone out of him, so that one wanted to know more. As I came to know, he was also a tough and a *stubborn* man, who was able to stand against public opinion and to talk about forgiveness through the dark and dangerous years of the war. In him those opposites had coincided.

In 1958 Dick Howard resigned to make way for a younger provost, and his resignation coincided with the arrival of a new bishop, Cuthbert Bardsley, a truly charismatic person, to lead us towards the consecration. In him, too, was that coincidence of opposites: he had a strong and rich ego, and the paradox between egocentricity and self abandon was daily being tested and resolved. Charismatic literally means one who accepts charis, the 'free gift' of grace. Cuthbert *accepted* his human nature as a free gift, gave *thanks* for it; then allowed this new self to be *broken* by the Spirit of Jesus, and that spirit to be *given* to others. It was this rhythm flowing through the personalities of Dick Howard and Cuthbert Bardsley which opened the way of consecration which now had to be enshrined in the new cathedral; it is the way which flowed through Jesus on that last night as he prayed 'for their sakes, I consecrate myself'.

The Bishop appointed five of us as midwives to bring this

truth to birth. First and foremost, a new provost, Bill Williams, a South African. Then a precentor, Joseph Poole, to guide the worship. Third and fourth, two canons, Edward Patey and Simon Phipps – Edward to work in the world of Education and Youth, and Simon in the world of Industry. The fifth, a chaplain to the cathedral, myself, to work as a 'diocesan missioner', and at the same time to be the vicar of a country parish, Leamington Hastings. I was uneasy about the title of Missioner, which I felt would give the impression of somebody who knew all the answers and was always talking. My hopes were the opposite, to be always listening, and sharing the deep questions which are in everyone's heart. As the day came near for my family to arrive in our new home, the Bishop wrote a letter which reveals the kind of leader he was. 'My very dear Stephen, this letter brings my love and thankfulness as you go forward into the new stage of your life's work. I know that you will bring a deep and highly valued contribution. Keep close to me – I need your prayers and counsel – and pray that we may all enter more deeply into the fellowship of the Holy Spirit. God bless you both, ever your affectionate friend and Bishop, Cuthbert Coventry'.

We moved into our new house at the end of October, to find the builders still in occupation, the roof off and covered with a tarpaulin, and no heating. I left Scilla to cope, with the three girls – Robin had gone to a boarding school – and sped off to a conference on my all important diocesan work. The next morning she caught up with me in a furious letter and a desperate cry for help, and I sped back again, a wiser man. She had jerked me away from the false perception that God lived chiefly in cathedrals, while my obligations to my wife and children were secondary. It transpired over the next four years that the real consecration of Coventry Cathedral depended on getting that right.

My family began to learn how grateful we can be to live in a village – for we were invited to make our home in our neighbours' house until the vicarage was ready for us – and grateful for the beautiful countryside and the farmland in which we had arrived. There were two pigs in the field next to the vicarage and they became our friends. We called them Hodder and Stoughton, after my first publisher. Most of all we could be grateful for the people amongst whom we were now living, strong individualists, but interacting as a community, and conscious of their history.

However, this led to problems. After the first week I asked the Churchwardens to call a meeting of the parochial Church Council. But what were we going to discuss? To everything I suggested they said 'No, impossible'. For example, Worship? No, that would reveal deep divisions between those who wanted change, and those who did not want change. What about the relations between Anglicans and Methodists? No! No!. A thousand times No!. That was the most difficult question of all. There was a Methodist Chapel in the parish, and a history of 150 years of division, complicated by intermarriage between the two congregations. But this was the bull we took by the horns. It was no good having grandiose schemes about consecrating a cathedral if we could not break the *mould* of history and *give* our Christian traditions to each other.

But the way of consecration is difficult; as Jesus warned us, it is through suffering into joy, and in the end through death into life. In the beginning it may be through tears into laughter, as we discovered when it occurred to us that in our farming community, the first step might be for Methodists

105

and Anglicans to eat their harvest supper together. Immediately we ran into a problem; the Methodists said that they would not come if there was beer, and the Anglicans said that they would not come if there was not beer. This apparently trivial obstacle touched something very deep in both our traditions. I tried to get round it by serving *Cydrax,* which was brown and sparkled; but this offended everybody. The Methodists thought that it was alcoholic, but the Anglicans knew that it wasn't. We talked this through during the following year, and came to the conclusion that there could perhaps be diversity in our unity. Neither side was 'right' or 'wrong', but both saw an aspect of God's truth. Could we think of some way in which we might respect each other's convictions? So on the second year of our united harvest supper we decided that alcohol would not officially be served, but that the church-wardens would privately bring in a barrel of beer which would stand on a side table, and anyone who wished could help themselves. By the third year this had become our united tradition, and we had begun to laugh about it. One or two brave spirits had even crossed the line – in both directions.

Meanwhile Bishop Cuthbert was meeting weekly with the Cathedral staff. How would we celebrate the consecration of our Cathedral? How could we become a people who not only acted out that consecration in our ritual, but let the reality of it enter into our lives with each other?

As Diocesan Missioner, this was the question I was asking, and asking it first of my fellow clergy. The Church of England clergy are divided into chapters of a dozen or more members, who, at that time, used to meet about once a month, to receive instructions from the Bishop, and to organise joint activities. Much of the time was spent binding and grousing about 'them' at the centre, and about 'the quota', the money which each parish was required to send to the diocese. I determined to go round the Chapters to meet the clergy, to talk as little as possible, and to listen carefully.

One of my first visits was to the Monks Kirby Chapter, on the 17th of February 1959, and it is here the story starts. 'We are faced with a great opportunity', said one of the clergy, 'in the consecration of our cathedral'. 'An opportunity for what?' someone asked. 'How can it be more than a great festival and a blowing of trumpets?' A discussion started, and we very soon came to see that what the Spirit of God wanted was not just a consecrated cathedral but a consecrated people living round it: a people in whom he could be alive. Then followed the second uncomfortable discovery that if there was to be a consecrated people, it would have to begin with ourselves.

So we decided to go away together for a 'quiet day', in order to ask the question, 'What, O Lord God, do you want the Monks Kirby Chapter to do now?'

We gathered in a country parish on a summer morning. The programme was Holy Communion, breakfast, Bible study and silence. Then lunch, and a time of discussion. We sat under a crab apple tree, and asked each other 'What answer has God given to our questions?' Nothing emerged very clearly till one man said: 'You know, it's very good to get together like this'. Everyone agreed, and an old priest bordering on his eightieth birthday said: 'I think we ought to do it every week'. The others laughed, for this was clearly impossible. Parish priests are far too busy. They knew they hadn't time to meet weekly, to pray together, to read the Bible together, to be silent, and to discuss.

But now the truth began to dawn. We had asked 'What do

107

you want us to do?', and the answer was simple, obvious, yet revolutionary and costly: 'Meet Weekly'. There could be no more talk of impossibility. They decided to meet the following Monday from 9 to 10 am, and every Monday morning for three months. After three months they would review the position.

But after three months the position was so changed as to be hardly recognisable. The chapter consisted no longer of isolated parish priests, each battling on heroically alone. It had become a team who knew one another, cared about one another, belonged to one another, and most important of all, had begun to admit to one another their own weaknesses. In the autumn of 1959 the Monks Kirby Chapter wrote to the Bishop and told him what was happening.

Meanwhile the Bishop had called a meeting of his staff, asking us to come away with him for three days, to live and eat and pray together, and to discuss how we should prepare for the consecration of the cathedral in 1962. At that meeting I made a report of the Monks Kirby discoveries, and urged the Bishop to lay upon the other Chapters that they should begin to organise themselves into a similar pattern. When I had finished there was a long silence. After a while the Bishop said 'No, I won't lay anything on. If this is really of the Holy Spirit, it will bubble up from underneath'. And the Archdeacon of Warwick, who was sitting next him added: 'From my slight acquaintance with the Holy Spirit I believe that He will not be stereotyped, and he will not be hurried'.

The Bishop suggested that the Chapter Clerk of Monks Kirby should write to all the other twelve Chapters, and ask for a chance to meet them and tell them our story. Eleven of them invited us – while in the twelfth, one parish priest

argued convincingly to his brethren that they were consecrated already, by their ordination vows and needed nothing
more. So eleven days of prayer took place that winter, often
in icy cold village churches. I remember one such day when
the Rural Dean marched up and down the aisle, stamping his
feet and beating his breast, not so much in an agony of
contrition as in a failure of circulation. This was no time of
emotion, but rather of honest men trying to discover what
the spirit of Jesus wanted them to do.

The conclusion they came to was, in every case, that they
were being commanded to *meet,* though in every case they
decided on a different pattern of meeting. By the spring of
1960 it was obvious that a radical new thing was stirring
amongst the clergy, and the Bishop decided that he must
gather us together and try to discover what the spirit had
been saying to us.

We met at Balliol College, Oxford, about 180 of us. We
told our story and drew out its meaning: 'one truth, so
crashingly platitudinous, that we kick ourselves and
wonder, how on earth we had the face to pose as Christian
leaders before we saw it. *A new commandment I give to
you that you love one another as I have loved you,* that is
with a deep self-giving compassion. Until we have frankly
faced our differences, and come to know and trust one
another, all our Church work is sounding brass and
clanging cymbals.'

We then examined a plan for the future, which was in
everybody's hands on a duplicated piece of paper. It
embodied the idea that when a stone falls into the centre of a
pond, the ripples expand over the surface in ever widening
circles. So a stone had fallen into the pool of our diocese,
and the first ripple had been the Monks Kirby clergy. Now,

we must plan for the gathering in of the laity, in three ever widening circles.

The second ripple, we suggested, might be groups of clergy and laity, meeting together from October 1960 to Easter 1961; three parishes might combine, with each parish priest bringing three lay people. Here are some notes of what people are saying:

'Get laity to tell us how they see the Church, and what needs doing. Listen before we talk. How can clergy and laity help one another? Get off our pedestals. Admit we are only on the threshold of understanding. Painful meeting necessary. Radical and revolutionary questions to be asked. Listen to criticism, accept and absorb it. Let LAY perspective be revealed. Let groups be open to the Spirit to make adventures [if led] in prayer and obedience.'

The result of this ripple, we hoped, would be four convinced people to go back together into each parish, where the vision had to be worked out.

In every parish the third ripple would emerge as a different plan according to its needs. But in general, we would listen to each other, and learn about our baptismal vows, and about prayer. If our discussions spilt over into evangelism, let it begin with the opposite of what is generally thought of as evangelism. Let us learn to listen. Evangelism begins with prayer, humility, listening and service. Let the world tell the Church – only then can we share the story of Jesus.

The fourth ripple would be the gathering up of the whole diocese in certain dramatic acts, culminating in the Consecration of the Cathedral, May 26th 1962.

All this would bring us to a starting point. What the fifth ripple would be, nobody could foresee. I find in my old battered copy of that conference paper these words scribbled: 'God alone knows'.

Over the next 18 months these hopes unfolded into experience, in every case richer than we could have foreseen.

The clergy/laity groups showed us that if we became twelve real people to each other, we could experience the presence of God in our midst.

Out of this experience we became aware of a work to be done, but that we were inadequate to do it. And so the groups were driven one by one to prayer; not the conventional prayer we had been used to – 'the vicar thanked the ladies who had so kindly provided the tea, and he closed with prayer' – but a prayer which arose out of the group themselves, and out of our deep need. So there began to emerge a new clergy/laity pattern. The laity needed the clergy as never before. They needed teaching. The clergy began to recognise themselves as teachers of an eager laity, standing beside them in their doubts, and understanding the problems of their working lives; but above all as men of prayer, supporting the laity and exploring the meaning of prayer with them.

The Parish Groups. This was the third ripple on the pond. Here is a glimpse of it from a new housing estate in the city of Coventry.

The vicar and the three who had been with him in the clergy/laity group met with their Parochial Church Council, after which he rang up a friend. 'I just had to talk to someone. This has been the most wonderful meeting since I was ordained.' They had hatched a plan by which ten laity would *become leaders of groups in their own houses.* They would invite their friends, and only ask the vicar to join them when they really needed him. Through the whole of that winter these groups met monthly, while the leaders met monthly with the vicar to prepare for their next session, and report to him how things were going.

But it would be wrong to suggest a success story. Other groups petered out. What cried aloud to us was that group discussion is by no means easy, and that we must learn a technique of leadership that blends speaking with listening, and that enables others both to speak and to listen, and so to *set free the truth of the spirit,* that can spring out of the heart of a company of friends.

We were now approaching the fourth ripple, which we had foreseen as certain dramatic events leading up to the Consecration of the Cathedral.

In a few weeks our new cathedral was to be consecrated, but something revolutionary had already happened. As St Paul wrote to the first Christians at Corinth, 'Surely you know that you are God's temple, where the spirit of God dwells', we ourselves could become the consecrated cathedral where God's spirit lived.

The Cross of Nails. We approached the last forty days with a mixture of excitement and alarm, for now the Cross of Nails was to be taken out of the old ruined cathedral, where it had stood since 1941 in front of the words 'Father forgive', and it was to be carried round all our parishes. This would be a pilgrimage, to last forty days and forty nights, during which there would be kept a continuous chain of prayer. Each parish, where the cross rested, would be a link in that chain, and while they prayed for us, the whole diocese would pray for them.

The cross of nails suggested the answer to our question 'how can we become a consecrated people?', for it showed us that life in the spirit had to be life through death. Sometimes by day, sometimes in the middle of the night, it was handed over from one parish to another with the words 'Receive this Cross of Nails, brought to you with love and prayers from the ruined sanctuary of our Cathedral Church. Cherish it as a token of the merciful forgiveness of God, declared to us in the Passion of our Saviour Jesus Christ. Watch about it, in prayer for one another'.

Meanwhile, in hundreds of churches, the people were preparing *to reaffirm their baptismal vows,* in words from the Methodist Covenant Service, set within the framework of the Holy Communion. We had prepared little replicas of the cross of nails to be given to each person after they had affirmed their vows, and we had guessed that 10,000 would be sufficient. But we had hopelessly underestimated. Caught up in the inspiration of those forty days and forty nights, people came in totally unexpected numbers. The priest reminded them of the New Covenant which Jesus had made with his disciples, and called upon them joyfully and solemnly to renew that covenant. He read the Gospel in which Jesus gave his New Commandment, 'that you love one another as I have loved you'. Then the people reaffirmed their baptismal vows; the priest affirmed the declaration made at his ordination, after which the people prayed for him. Then they all knelt together in silence, and after a while joined together in the words ' I am no longer my own but thine ... put me to doing, put me to suffering ... I freely and heartily yield all things to thy pleasure and disposal. Amen,' Then followed the Holy Communion, and the remembrance of the moment when Jesus consecrated Himself.

On the night of May 24th 1962 this service was held in
many parish churches, including St John's Coventry, at the
opposite end of the shopping precinct to the Cathedral,
where the Cross of Nails was resting for the last hours of its
pilgrimage. As the service ended, the cross was carried out
of the church to where the Bishop was waiting to receive it,
accompanied by a great crowd from the other city parishes.
He himself, as Father of the family, carried it on that first
stage of the journey back to the Mother Church. The proces-
sion could hardly push its way through the crowds that had
gathered, and when they reached the ruins of the old
cathedral, where the cross had stood for so many years, they
found it packed with people from wall to wall. Then the
cross was handed back to the Provost and carried into the
new cathedral to be set in position above the high altar at the
centre of the diocese: the symbol of our life together in the
Spirit, but at the same time of life through death – the
symbol of those opposites – the symbol of the glory of God.

This is not the place to describe May 25th 1962. But
certain moments live in the memory: the moment of
Consecration itself when, with drums rolling and a fanfare
of trumpets, the choirs sang Alleluia! Alleluia! Alleluia!
And the congregation burst into a hymn of praise. But the
greatest moment of all came the next morning, when the
Bishop stood at the heart of his diocese, and taking a little
loaf of bread in his hands repeated the age long words:
'Who in the same night that He was betrayed, took bread,
and when he had given thanks, He broke it, and gave it to
His disciples ...'

As the prayer ended, the trumpets sounded, and there
followed a profound silence.

*

During the next three weeks we experienced an outburst of worship and happiness as the whole diocese celebrated a festival.

Great services were held in the new cathedral offering up to God every part of our daily lives – services for Industry and Agriculture, for Schools, the Medical Services, the Armed Forces, Local Government, Youth, Old Age Pensioners, to mention only a few. There were services of International Reconciliation when young people of many nations asked the burning questions that confronted their generation, and when church leaders from many countries and denominations knelt before the great tapestry of Christ reigning in glory, and prayed for His forgiveness and for the coming of His kingdom.

Many of the acts of worship were created by artists. There was the first performance of Benjamin Britten's *War Requiem,* that work of unbelievable power and beauty and insight, where the futility of war is set against the eternal mercy of God. Sung under the compassionate gaze of the Christ who looks down from Graham Sutherland's tapestry it summed up and expressed the meaning of the Cathedral. After the performance, Sir Basil Spence the architect, and Benjamin Britten the composer, met, and both deeply moved, thanked each other. 'Thank you for your Cathedral in which my Requiem could be performed'. 'Thank you for your Requiem, sung in my Cathedral'. Through the inspiration of those two men and the travail of their fellow artists a beauty had been born and a truth spoken.

Many of the artists who performed in the Cathedral during those weeks were caught up into the glory. Yehudi Menuhin, standing alone in the chancel, seemed to shine and become transfigured, and to be one with his violin and with the music that poured out of him. Edric Conner, going up to sing, whispered 'pray for me', and then sang with such electrifying power, of Jesus rescuing a soul from hell, that 2,000 people gripped their chairs in terror and relief, and he himself returned to his seat trembling and pouring with sweat.

The same inspiration, the same liberating power, was experienced by visitors to other parts of the diocese. A speaker from London wrote 'I spoke to those people, from the other end of the diocese from the new Cathedral, as I did not know I could speak. I had wanted to be sick the minute before. Now I knew just what I must say, and said it simply and clearly ... We had seen a glimpse of the beginnings of the church. How precious the grace! How feeble our love! I too, you see, was being consecrated'.

WINDSOR

After some years at Coventry I was appointed as a Canon of Windsor. The job was partly to preside over the worship in St George's House. This was a college, established a few years earlier to run courses for Clergy and Laity. Our prime task was to provide training for promising clergy in their forties. They were invited to come and stay with us for some weeks to share their ideas, hopes and aspirations. As time went on, we agreed to extend the courses to clergy in their fifties who were beginning to think back upon their ministries and face new challenges ahead. Such groups were fertile soil for planting and nourishing ideas about the potential for growth and human fulfilment.

Many other kind of people also began to come to St George's House – prominent people from the world of politics, spiritual leaders of different faiths and people who wanted to talk about the social changes which were affecting our daily lives. There was a wide spectrum of questions and opinions from such people as Arthur Scargill and the Dalai Lama, actors, musicians, leaders of our armed forces, prison governors, chief constables and many more representatives of the society in which we live. These diverse groups presented new challenges to my language, when theological insights were allowed to enter into the debate. I began to think deeply about my use of the word 'God'. People would often say to me that they did not believe in God, and when I asked them what it was that they did not believe, I usually kept on my response of saying 'I, too, do not believe in that kind of God'.

So what is it that I do believe? The short answer must be Love – but Love wearing three masks, like the actors in times past – three persons, the Father, the Son and the Holy Spirit and the dance of Love between them.

Life at Windsor was rich, exciting, intense, hectic and demanding. It was also a difficult time for me, personally. My dear wife, Scilla, was found to have cancer and after a while, she died. In the depths of mourning I immersed myself into writing my third book – Into the New Age – as a tribute to Scilla. I explored and reflected in depth what it is to be human, how joy and sadness are interwoven, how life and death are intertwined, and how St John's 'eis ton aiona' reveals to us a new possibility of being human.

I cannot conclude my account of being at Windsor without some appreciation of the Queen, whose presence transformed the lives of so many of the people who lived there. Windsor has been her home for over 50 years, and she has, here, an enormous extended family with whom she continues to be concerned.

Here are two glimpses of that concern.

The first was when she gave a tea party for the military knights and distinguished ex service men, who lived in a row of houses opposite The Chapel. One of the military knights had recently been discharged from hospital, and when the Queen arrived, he was finding it quite painful to be standing. The Queen noticed this and invited him to sit down. He immediately said 'I cannot sit in your presence, your Majesty', to which the Queen replied 'It's an order'. So he sat, doubly happy to rest his body, and to obey an order from his Commander in Chief.

The second glimpse arose out of my own sorrow. A few weeks after my dear wife, Scilla, had died, I received an invitation to have dinner with the Queen. When I arrived, I discovered, to my surprise, that I was guest of honour and should be sitting at the Queen's right side. We took our places, and the first course was a dish of caviar sent by the Shah of Persia to the Queen of England. The dish came to me first, as guest of honour, and I had to confess to the Queen that I had no idea how much to take because I had never before had caviar. She graciously came to my help and we were both amused. This little incident led to a deep conversation between us about my agony at the death of my wife, and her agony at the death of her father.

The next day there was a note from the Queen, written in her own hand, giving me the name and address of another bereaved person she had recently met, whom she felt I might like to talk with, and he with me.

A BISHOP

꧁❧꧂

In 1977 I was consecrated as Bishop of Repton in Derbyshire. I prepared for my consecration by going to stay with Jean Vanier's L'Arche Community in France.

When I retired nine years later, somebody asked me 'What have been the highlights?'

My answer, which was at least half true, was that everything had been lit by a highlight.

But there were two events which I remember with special vividness, both outside the ecclesiastical structure, and in which I was acting out of the truth of Consecration, though I did not understand this at the time. The first concerned a coal strike; the second, a marriage.

The Coal Strike

In 1984 violent clashes broke out between the police and the miners who had set up pickets to enforce a strike in protest against the threatened closure of their pits. Derbyshire was one of the centres of coal mining in the country, and anger was running high. Parish priests were being tested in their ministry to families who were being torn apart by dissension between fathers and sons. I sensed that the Church might be able to do something towards a reconciliation. But what? So I arranged to meet with a few officials from the Coal Board, and listened to their case. In brief, the pits must be closed because they didn't pay. Then I arranged to meet with officials from the Union and listened to their case. They claimed that they had not been consulted, that closure was far more than an economic issue and that alternatives to closure were possible. Then I suggested that the two groups should meet each other. At first this was flatly rejected by the Coal Board group who saw the miners as troublemakers; and by the miners' group who were convinced that the Coal Board were not to be trusted, and must be forced by strike action. Eventually they both yielded to persuasion and agreed to meet, provided it could be in secret.

So we approached an elderly lady who had a flat in the middle of the mining area, and she agreed to let us use it for a meeting. We arrived, unofficially, one evening. We were all very suspicious of each other, but each side succeeded in expressing their point of view, and at the end we agreed to meet again. As we were leaving the flat one of the Coal Board's toughest executives said to me 'I don't see what good these meetings are going to do'; and I replied 'Neither do I'. This shook him to the roots. He imagined that anyone convening such a meeting must have a plan, but I genuinely had no plan – except that we should meet. Then, as we said goodbye, he shook me to the roots, by saying 'If anyone reveals that this meeting has happened, I shall deny that I was here'. His name was Ken Moses, and during the following years right up to his death, he became a close friend.

We held two or three more meetings in that lady's flat and gradually we moved towards trusting each other.

If both sides could listen to the other's point of view, then it might be possible to begin a conversation. As we listened to the Coal Board we understood that the pits had to make a profit. As wc listened to the miners we began to appreciate their history, culture and the skills inherited from their fathers, and how they proudly resisted the idea of being subsidised. But it appeared to them that Mrs Thatcher was unaware of all this. I wrote to her and told her about the concerns of the miners, and got a long and thoughtful, but unyielding, letter in reply.

I also went to visit the Secretary of the National Union of Mineworkers who received me in a friendly fashion at his home in Derbyshire and offered me a gin and tonic. But when I went to meet him in London, in confidence, with Arthur Scargill, he behaved evasively and excused himself from any further discussions.

I got the impression that the protagonists, Margaret Thatcher and Arthur Scargill were each caught up in a competitive system where there had to be a 'winner'. Any kind of reconciliation could not be part of their agenda. In fact, 20 years later, a form of reconciliation was achieved when, in at least one coalfield, the whole area of the coal mine was given over to creating a new town. Resources and opportunities, so conspicuously absent from the old mining villages, were introduced and the local people were consulted and involved in the planning.

As I reflected on the deadlock between Mrs Thatcher and Arthur Scargill, I began to understand that reconciliation reflects common sense – something apparently unavailable to these two people. Common sense calls out for divergent thinking. We are all different, and need each other. It is absurd to think that I am right and everybody else is wrong. I am right, and *at the same time* wrong . The coincidence of opposites begins inside myself; the only way to cope with it is to accept the ambiguity, and then to give thanks for it and to allow forgiveness, compassion and reconciliation to unfold. To embrace diversity in unity is common sense.

But reconciliation is not always immediately possible for men and women who live in clock time. We have to make choices, and commit ourselves to one or other course. The great world religions recognise this dilemma, and the way forward which they advocate begins with a change of mind, called repentance – a new way of seeing God and each other.

Part of this change of mind is to see in myself and in each other the climax, the ladder on which messengers go up and come down between the reality of time and the reality of Eternity. And at the same time, to recognise in each of us the subtle snake.

I see in retrospect that both the Coal Board and the Union officials recognised that the issue was, indeed, one of economics, but at the same time, one of people; and how a Bishop representing both sides of this dilemma, might have become the ambassador of 'a change of mind', on the basis of which they could begin a conversation.

Marriage, Life and Death

In 1976, while I was still a Canon of Windsor, I went on a short holiday to Istanbul with two of my daughters, Helen and Katharine. There, on the first evening, in the foyer of The Pera Palace Hotel, I met someone called Sandra. I was surprised to see that she was reading Daniel Deronda by George Eliot, because I, too, was reading the same book. I also became intrigued when I saw that she was writing postcards in Welsh and learned that she used to teach Latin, Greek and Art through the medium of Welsh in a school in mid Wales. My father's family had strong Welsh connections, and we had an exceptional collection of Welsh Bibles at my family home in Buckinghamshire. My father had

learnt Welsh, and I, as a boy of five had learned to sing a
song in Welsh. I did not know, that evening in Istanbul, that
soon, I was to become Bishop of Repton, and would be
representing that precious branch of Christianity – the Early
Celtic Church – a church which, today, people are increas-
ingly learning to appreciate because of its simplicity,
divergent thinking and true sophistication.

Sandra took us all to a shop which sold the best Turkish
Delight in Istanbul, and on our return to England, she and I
continued to meet.

Five years later we were married. But in the meantime I
had myself become a Bishop, and my marriage was contro-
versial because Sandra had been divorced. I was the
Suffragan Bishop of Repton, in the diocese of Derby, and my
Diocesan Bishop, Cyril Bowles, helped me to sort out the
legal position, After much discussion we came to the conclusion that the marriage would not be illegal by ecclesiastical
law; but that, at the same time, it would cause distress to
some of our church colleagues, who would see it as under-
mining the sanctity of marriage. Sandra had been abandoned
by Peter, her sculptor husband, and had lived alone for ten
years. I, as a widower, had lived alone for seven years.
Neither of us had divorced anyone, but we both felt a sense
of sadness regarding our first marriages, because we had not
loved well enough. It seemed to be a decision between law
and grace, and, in the end, to call in question Jesus Christ
'full of grace and truth' and the reality of the forgiveness of
sin. The word for 'sin', in the original Greek means to miss
the target; we as human beings fail to live up to Jesus' New
Commandment – 'Love one another as I have loved you.' But
Jesus forgives, and offers us a new start. I see, in retrospect,
that to accept that offer with gratitude, was probably our best

possible witness to the truth of Christian marriage, and to its foundation in grace and truth.

During the two years prior to our marriage we had private discussions with a huge number of people both inside and outside the structures of the Church. On a personal level, the most important discussion I had, outside the Church, was with Peter, Sandra's first husband. On meeting, we liked each other immediately, but he challenged some of my ideas about marriage, divorce and 'relationships ending'. He seemed to be able to hold together with respect both their marriage and their divorce, because, in unison, they had led him to a third relationship with Sandra – the one they had *now* – which he greatly valued. Peter died around a decade later, and I had the privilege of officiating at his immensely inspiring funeral, based around the writings of James Joyce. The following year Sandra and I were honoured guests of The Welsh Arts Council at Peter's Retrospective Exhibition in Cardiff.

Within the structures of the Church, I had, eventually, after great agonising, decided that I *had* to marry Sandra, and that it would be a sin if I did *not* marry her. I wrote to Robert Runcie, the then Archbishop of Canterbury, to tell him what I was intending to do. I said that I only wished to inform him and that I was not asking him to comment. I also wrote in confidence to all my fellow bishops informing them of my decision.

The question then arose, where should we be married and by whom? Sandra was a Welsh Baptist, and it seemed that the natural thing to do would be to be married in her home church in Wales. So, in 1981, on a May morning, we were married in a little white washed chapel, by a stream, in a wood near the village of Bethlehem in West Wales. The sun came out after a shower, and the trees and flowers sparkled with raindrops. We were married by her Minister, John Young, and the service was conducted partly in Welsh and partly in English. Bishop Cyril celebrated Holy Communion, and Hugh Montefiore, the Bishop of Birmingham, read from the gospel of St John. It was a moment of pure happiness, when each of us could know once again 'I am loved and I love'. It was one of those moments when eternal life is NOW. We promised to love and to cherish till death us do part.

But life was not going to be easy. Soon after our wedding we discovered the joy of Sandra being pregnant, but the following March, after a wonderful pregnancy, the consultant recognised an emergency. The baby, a little boy, was induced. He appeared to be beautifully perfect but was found to have an incurable heart disorder. He lived for one day, and the only events of his little life were that he was given the name of Harry Stephen by his parents, baptised by his father, and died in his mother's arms.

Some weeks later, early on a Sunday morning, I was looking out into the garden, and I saw a sheep with a little black lamb. There had never been a sheep in our garden before, and never again since that morning. It was more or less impossible for sheep to have strayed into our garden. I went outside, but they had gone leaving their footprints in the soil. It was the fortieth day since Harry's death – the day on which the soul is set free to enter into a new relationship with heaven and earth, as happened to Jesus.

I went back into the house, and looked at the gospel {the good news} appointed for that day. It was from St John Chapter 10, where Jesus says 'I AM the good shepherd, and I AM the door, through which the sheep go out and come in', the door between time and eternity.

126

I found Sandra and told her what I had seen in the garden. She immediately said that she had always thought of Harry as a little black Welsh lamb, and then I remembered the dress woven out of black Welsh sheep's wool which I had had made for her when we became engaged. I cannot say 'it was as though Harry had come to tell his parents that he was alive and happy and cared for'. He had *really* come, using a language which would make sense to his mother and father on that particular morning in time. He was saying to us 'in my human body you literally became one flesh. NOW. I AM the good shepherd, I AM the door that has brought me to you out of eternity, so that in my spirit and in His Spirit you may become one, for in eternity there are no dividing walls of opposites.

It is not sentimental nonsense to believe that Jesus brought Harry into our garden that morning. We might ask how could he have time to shepherd everyone of the millions of souls who pass through death every day? But as a friend of mine, Julia de Beausobre, once said to me, 'the moment of death will be the inrush of timelessness'. Remembering that morning, Sandra and I saw together the backside of eternity which had passed by.

If we ask God 'show us who you are', he might reply, as Jesus said to the woman at the well, 'go and fetch your husband and come back'. He might say to us, 'look inside your marriage, at the to and fro of love between husband and wife'. Above all he would say 'a new commandment I have given to you. Love one another as I have loved you'.

Love is far more than the upsurge of sexual attraction; Love is woven into its opposites; Love leads through failure and suffering, and teaches us the meaning of compassion and forgiveness; Love is stronger than death.

POSTSCRIPT
Sandra Verney

꧁꧂

In 1986, at the age of 67, Stephen began his active retirement.

There were many big issues facing the church, and he wanted to set up a centre where opposing points of view could be properly debated. A few generous friends raised the money to buy The Abbey at Sutton Courtenay in Oxfordshire. It had a wonderful medieval hall, plenty of accommodation and beautiful grounds, near the heart of the village.

Here, he and Fred Blum set up a community which was to be rooted in Christianity, but open to the wisdom of other faiths. Fred was a psychoanalyst by profession and a Jew by birth and by faith. But, over the next few years he became an Anglican. He was confirmed by Stephen during the early hours of an Easter Day at Fairacres Convent in Oxford. He was later ordained, and became a parish priest in Oxfordshire. Then tragically, he died, and the world was deprived of one of its most original personalities.

Meanwhile, at The Abbey, a community had become established on a basis of daily prayer, meditation and a weekly eucharist. The Abbey was now able to host people who wanted somewhere where they could go to stop and think.

Interfaith groups came together to confront the issues which concerned them all – Roman Catholics, Southern Baptists, Orthodox, Methodists, Moslems, Bahais, Zoroastrians, Jews, Buddhists and Jains . Anglicans of all persuasions came to discuss the problems in their own church.

One of the best publications concerning the ordination of women to the priesthood, '**A Fearful Symmetry**' emerged as a result of people with opposing views coming to meet, listen and talk to each other.

The Church's Energy Group was started in the mid 1980s, Eminent nuclear physicists, Green Peace and Friends of the Earth held regular meetings to voice their deep concern about global climate change and the government's lack of attention to the matters that have, since, become part of our daily vocabulary.

These are just a few of the struggles that became part of The Abbey, and they lead us firmly back to Stephen's third image at the beginning of this book. The people who came to The Abbey were sometimes reluctant to meet with their 'opposites', as indeed many of us are. But as time went on what often emerged was that the 'opposites', while remaining separate, were being picked up and held together by some kind of love and respect, which allowed the occasional glimpse of God's truth on the other side of Nicholas of Cusa's garden wall.

Lightning Source UK Ltd.
Milton Keynes UK
UKHW021508111022
410297UK00002B/592